# Earth Everyday

**Small Steps Towards a Greener Tomorrow**

by
**Henley Turner**

ISBN-13: (hardcover)
ISBN-13: (paperback)
ISBN-13: (ebook)
ISBN-13: (audiobook)

Dear Esteemed Reader,

**Thank you immensely for choosing this book to join your collection.** We imagine that you've already embarked on an exploration of ideas within these pages, and we couldn't be happier about it!

Now, if you find yourself chuckling, pondering, or even debating with the words in front of you, we'd absolutely love to hear about it. If you can spare a few moments to pen down your thoughts in a review, we would be as delighted as a dictionary on a spelling bee!

An Amazon review would be excellent - but hey, we're far from picky. Whether it's a scribble on the back of a grocery list, a tweet, or even a message in a bottle (though that might take a while to reach us), your feedback is gold.

Writing a review might not be as fun as a spontaneous dance-off, but we promise it'll bring grins to our faces, warmth to our hearts, and incredibly valuable insights to future readers.

With Gratitude,

Bo Bennett, PhD
Publisher
Archieboy Holdings, LLC.

# Table of Contents

# Introduction:
# Embracing a Greener Lifestyle

In an epoch where the whispers of our planet's distress have crescendoed into a roar impossible to ignore, the notion of a greener lifestyle has shifted from a casual consideration to a critical imperative. What once seemed like a mere choice of preference has now become a clarion call for action—a push for immediate and meaningful change in how we live, consume, and coexist with the delicate ecosystems around us. As we stand at this crossroads, it becomes evident that individual actions, no matter how seemingly modest, coalesce into the collective power necessary to forge substantial transformations.

The evidence of humanity's impact on the Earth is unequivocal, the data irrefutable. No longer can we afford to be mere bystanders in the unfolding narrative of ecological shift. Our daily choices, habits, and routines are threads intertwined in the larger tapestry of environmental health. This introduction does not dwell on the specific science of impending ecological thresholds—those are expounded upon in the chapters that follow—but rather, it seeks to ignite a genuine, heartfelt pursuit for sustainability in our everyday lives. It is about a resolve borne not from fear, but from an informed awareness and a hopeful vision for the world we want to inhabit and pass on to future generations.

By stepping into the world of green living, we uncover a spectrum of opportunities to reduce our ecological footprint. From the simplicity of mindful recycling to the enriching practice of composting; from the crucial act of conserving water to the foundational challenge of reducing waste. Each chapter of this journey elucidates not just the 'what' and the 'why,' but the 'how'—providing practical, executable strategies tailored for the busiest of lives.

Embracing an eco-conscious lifestyle isn't just about individual habit adjustments—it's an invitation to join a growing, global throng of voices and forces standing up for a planet under siege. It is about traversing the distance from concern to action, from inertia to momentum. Adjustments to our dietary choices, being conscious of energy use, and supporting secondhand markets are all cogs in the wheel of positive change. We begin by planting seeds of sustainability in the gardens of our homes, and we watch them grow into a forest of change capable of sheltering future generations.

This introduction, and the chapters that follow, is a tapestry of information, inspiration, and invitation. It's time to weave our individual threads into a collective quilt of resiliency and reverence for nature. As we flip through the pages of possibility, let us embark on an transformative journey towards preserving our home, our planet. Let us embrace the greener lifestyle with intention, with action, and with hope for the thriving future we all deserve.

# Chapter 1:
# The Precipice of Change

As we segue from contemplating the myriad ways our planet speaks through its discomfort—eco-systemic shifts and extreme weather events—it's evident we stand on the precipice of change. Humanity has carved its mark upon the Earth with a heavy hand, altering landscapes and influencing climates in ways that have awakened a global reckoning. Within the pages of this chapter, we delve into the stark reality of our impact on Earth, measuring the weight of our ecological footprint against the fragile scales of nature. We explore the ticking countdown clock, assessing the years scientists suggest we may have left to rectify our course before we reach irreversible tipping points. This chapter does not venture into lamentations but serves as a cornerstone to understand the imperative of action. It's a rallying cry to recognize our collective responsibility and the transformational potential of informed, concerted effort. With clarity, purpose, and an unwavering commitment to the environment, let us embark on a journey towards sustainability rooted in knowledge and guided by the understanding that each choice we make is a thread in the fabric of our planetary future.

## Understanding Our Impact on the Planet

The pages behind us have painted a narrative of urgency, an imperative call to acknowledge our place at the precipice of an era demanding change. As we delve into the fabric of this chapter, let's embark on a reflective journey—a discerning examination of how our actions have, and continue to, profoundly affect the biosphere that sustains us all. It is from this understanding that we can then surmise how even the smallest of individual efforts can foster a larger, more significant transformation.

In our modern times, the human imprint on the natural world has reached unprecedented levels. From the air we breathe to the depths of our oceans, the impact is all-encompassing. Greenhouse gases suffuse the atmosphere, insulating the planet and spurring climate irregularities. Each puff from a car's exhaust, every coal plant's billowing plume, contributes to this expansive global issue. Our carbon footprint leaves an indelible mark, influencing climate patterns and ecosystems alike.

The intricacies of our planet work akin to an elaborate symphony, with each species and habitat contributing its own unique note. Yet, humankind has played the discordant instrument, prompting the loss of biodiversity at a rate that mirrors the great extinctions of our planet's past. Where ancient woodland once stood, urbanization sprawls; where coral reefs once thrived, bleached skeletons remain—a stark reminder of the aquatic life they once supported.

Our waterways tell a similar tale. Once-pristine rivers and streams now grapple with pollution—from industrial discharge to plastic debris—the ramifications of which cascade through the food web. Marine creatures mistake microplastics for sustenance, ingesting toxic particles that have journeyed from our hands to the furthest reaches of the oceanic expanse. Our interconnectedness with these systems is undeniable; the health of our waters reflects back upon the health of our communities.

Within the soil beneath our feet, human activities such as over-farming and deforestation have led to degradation, robbing the earth of nutrients and disrupting the delicate balance needed to sustain flourishing ecosystems. Soil erosion leads to diminished crop productivity and contributes to food insecurity, an issue that holds the potential to ripple across continents, affecting millions.

The agricultural practices that fill our plates also play a significant role in our planetary impact. Industrial farming operations, especially those catering to meat and dairy production, utilize copious amounts of water and land resources. The offshoot of these practices is not solely what lies on the dinner table, but rather, an assortment of by-products, such as methane, a potent greenhouse gas, and nitrogen-rich runoff that eutrophies bodies of water, inducing algal blooms and dead zones.

Additionally, the consumption culture fostered by modern society fuels a cycle of production, waste, and pollution. Fast fashion casts off fleeting trends in exchange for grounded ecosystems, and electronic waste deposits hazardous materials in lands far from where they originated. The obsolescence built into many products drives a relentless extraction of resources, disregarding the finite nature of raw materials vested within the Earth.

Our energy demands have similarly etched a significant mark on the planet. Fossil fuel extraction and consumption have not only spurred climate change but have also led to oil spills, air pollution, and the disruption of land and communities. The shift to renewable energy sources shines as a beacon of progress but is accompanied by its own set of complexities that must be navigated thoughtfully.

Despite this litany of impacts, there is room for optimism. Awareness is spreading, and with it, a burgeoning conscientiousness about the environment. This growing understanding translates into increased demand for sustainable practices and products, powering the economy of the future, one that prizes longevity and stewardship over short-term gain. It is a pivotal moment where understanding morphs into action, where each individual's choices become part of a collective surge towards betterment.

To conceive the vastness of our impact on the planet can be daunting, yet, in recognizing our role, we embrace the potential for change. We are a species of extraordinary adaptability, capable of innovation and altruism. By rethinking the ways we produce and consume; by advocating for policies and technologies that defend the biosphere; by nurturing a deep-seated respect for the living world—we embolden a movement towards lasting, positive change.

Our individual actions, when multiplied on a global scale, can mitigate our environmental footprints. Choices like diminishing energy consumption within our homes, curating more plant-based diets, and opting for modes of transport less reliant on fossil fuels are but a few examples of how we can forge a new path, one that veers away from environmental degradation and towards regeneration.

Without question, it is a monumental task, this shifting of course towards sustainability. Yet, history is replete with examples of humanity overcoming seemingly insurmountable challenges through ingenuity and resilience. We find ourselves at a junction where inaction translates to complicity in the demise of ecosystems. The call to action is clear and immediate; our moment to make a difference is now.

We stand not just at the precipice of change, but at the dawn of realization—the recognition that each day presents an opportunity to choose differently, to live in a manner that honors and protects the world we are part of. It begins with understanding, with the acknowledgment of the magnitude of our impact on the planet—a foundation upon which we can build a legacy of environmental stewardship for generations to come.

As the following chapters unfold, they will not only examine the ticking countdown of our planet's health but also empower us with practical, everyday strategies to contribute to its wellness. As stewards of the Earth, we hold the privilege and the responsibility to ensure its vibrancy, so that its verdant forests, its teeming oceans, and its diverse creatures may flourish. It is a profound duty—one that we embrace with open hearts and determined minds.

Let us continue this journey with eyes wide open to the realities we face and hearts full of the resolve needed to enact change. The preservation of our planet hangs in balance, and the weight of action rests upon all shoulders. Together, we can pivot from the brink, from the precipice of change, and venture towards a future where nature and humanity thrive in concert. The path ahead is ours to forge, step by conscientious step.

**The Countdown Clock: How Many Years Left?** As we turn the page from understanding our impact on the planet, a pressing question stands forefront in our minds: how many years do we have left to make significant changes before the damage to our Earth becomes irreversible? The stark reality is that our global timeline is not defined by centuries or even multiple generations ahead, but is measured in a handful of decades – or even less.

Scientists continuously analyze and update their projections, but a consensus underscores a critical point: we are fast approaching a tipping point. These scientists warn that if we do not drastically alter our current trajectory within the next decade, we will set into motion a series of catastrophic environmental events from which we may not be able to recover.

The Intergovernmental Panel on Climate Change (IPCC), an authoritative voice on climate science, provides assessments that encapsulate the urgency of our situation. Their reports conclude that we have until 2030 to make unprecedented and far-reaching changes across all facets of society to limit global warming to 1.5 degrees Celsius above pre-industrial levels.

This deadline is not an arbitrary one; the threshold of 1.5 degrees Celsius is a critical marker. Beyond this, we anticipate more frequent and severe weather events, loss of species, and depletion of natural resources – all contributing to a decline in global health and economy.

A mere half-degree beyond this target could mean a significant increase in water scarcity, extreme heat, and a substantial increase in people exposed to climate-related risks and poverty.

Part of what makes this countdown so pressing is the inertia built into the Earth's climatic systems. Greenhouse gases like carbon dioxide have long-lasting effects, meaning today's emissions will continue to warm the planet for centuries to come. Even if we halted all emissions tomorrow, the gases already in the atmosphere would continue to drive climate impacts for generations.

It is not just the air temperature and weather patterns that are of concern, either. Our oceans are acidifying at a rate that threatens marine life, irreversible melting of ice caps is causing sea-level rise, and the loss of biodiversity is so profound that some liken it to a sixth mass extinction.

Yet, the countdown clock is not merely a harbinger of doom; it serves as a compelling call to action. In this urgent context, individual and collective decisions have enormous power. The speed at which we transition to renewable sources of energy, the efficiency with which we manage our resources, and the sustainability of our consumption patterns will all have a profound impact on slowing down the countdown clock.

In confronting this deadline, it is essential to maintain a clear-eyed approach. While the timeframe is alarmingly short, it is also an opportunity to initiate profound and positive change. Progress is possible through technological innovation, policy reform, and societal transformation. This change demands not only awareness and education but ambition and courage to act quickly.

As this countdown continues, the need for solutions has moved beyond preventative measures to include adaptive strategies that mitigate the effects of climate change already set in motion. Cities are fortifying themselves against rising sea levels and storms, and agriculture is adapting to shifting growing seasons.

In conclusion, the answer to our chapter's titular question is contingent upon our actions today. While we cannot predict the exact number of years we have left before reaching irreversible thresholds, we can actively engage in extending this timeline and reshaping our future. In the following chapters, we will explore tangible steps that can be taken to stave off this relentless countdown and pave the way for a more sustainable world.

# Chapter 2:
# The Power of Everyday Choices

As we stand at the precarious edge explored in our initial discourse, it's paramount to recognize that the power to steer us back to safety lies not solely in grandiose acts but in the seemingly negligible decisions we make each day. From the selection of a bamboo toothbrush over plastic, to opting for public transport or carpooling, these choices, amassed over time and populations, become the very levers capable of shifting our environmental trajectory. These minute, conscious decisions are the unsung heroes in our quest for sustainability; they weave an intricate tapestry of small, purposeful actions that collectively create a substantial impact. Each sip from a refillable water bottle, every conscientious purchase we make, and the steadfast refusal to succumb to the convenience of disposable culture—these are the silent, yet powerful statements we cast for the future we yearn to realize. In acknowledging the gravity each choice carries, we awaken to the fact that our daily rituals are deeply interlinked with the fate of our shared home, Earth. Thus, the tapestry we craft can either smother or enliven the planet we so dearly cherish.

## Simple Shifts for Significant Outcomes

Embedded within the rhythm of our everyday existence are patterns, practices, and preferences that hold the power to greatly influence the health and future of our planet. It's not about grand gestures or monumental sacrifices, but rather the small, mindful adjustments we integrate into the fabric of our daily routines that can yield substantial environmental results.

Sometimes it's as simple as starting the day right. For instance, imagine the morning routine—one that often includes brewing a cup of coffee. Consider swapping disposable coffee pods for a reusable filter or purchasing beans from a local roaster who prioritizes sustainable sourcing. This seemingly minor choice could curtail waste and support responsible cultivation practices.

Transportation, often a necessity, is another area ripe for change. While electric cars and bike-to-work schemes are commendable, not everyone can access or afford them. Yet, consolidating errands to reduce trips or carpooling with coworkers are shifts that not only cut down on emissions but can strengthen community bonds as well.

The meals we consume carry their own weight in environmental impact. Adding one meatless meal a week, a concept known as "Meatless Monday," can significantly reduce carbon and water footprints. The collective effort of individuals taking part in this movement has the potential to lead to sizeable environmental improvements.

Consider the products that festoon our bathroom shelves—shampoos, soaps, cleansers. Opting for bar soaps and shampoos without plastic packaging, or purchasing from companies that offer refills can notably decrease the amount of plastic waste generated from personal care products.

In the sphere of technology, our appetite for the latest gadgets accelerates not only consumption but also electronic waste. By resisting the urge for constant upgrades and opting for repaired or refurbished electronics, we not only prolong the life cycle of our devices but also contribute less to the swelling tide of electronic waste.

Fashion, too, has its role in this narrative. The textile industry is notorious for pollution and waste. Shifting to a quality-over-quantity mindset, choosing sustainable brands, or engaging in the circular economy through second-hand shopping can drastically reduce the environmental footprint of our wardrobes.

At home, the power to shape outcomes is just as potent. Simple actions such as turning off lights when not in use, opting for energy-efficient LED bulbs, or investing in smart power strips that reduce phantom energy draw can noticeably lower energy consumption.

In the grocery aisles, choices also abound. Opting for bulk purchases reduces packaging waste, and bringing reusable bags and containers is a direct action against the pervasive issue of plastic pollution. The collective result of these choices can lead to a cleaner, less cluttered environment.

The office environment should not escape this scrutiny. Encouraging a culture of printing less, reusing stationery, and going digital where possible, are all steps that can lead to a significant reduction in resource consumption and waste.

Even our leisure activities offer avenues for action. Engaging in outdoor recreation that does not require motorized equipment not only reduces greenhouse gas emissions, but also nurtures an appreciation for the natural environment, further inspiring conservation efforts.

Financial decisions are equally impactful. Investing in green stocks or supporting crowdfunded environmental projects provides capital for sustainable innovations and signals to the market that there is a demand for green solutions.

Education plays a crucial role as well. By staying informed about environmental issues and sharing knowledge with peers, a culture of sustainability can be fostered. This knowledge can be as simple as understanding which plastics are recyclable, to recognizing the broader implications of climate policy decisions.

Finally, the adage 'reduce, reuse, recycle' holds enduring wisdom. Prioritizing the reduction of consumption and the extension of the lifespan of items through reuse are vital complements to recycling efforts. As societies, we must transition from linear models of consumption to embracing circular economies where the value of materials and resources is maximized, and waste is designed out of the system.

As these examples illustrate, the power of personal choice is immeasurable. It is through the aggregation of countless acts by individuals across the globe that we can begin to steer the colossal ship of environmental change. Simple shifts, when multiplied by the millions, can lead to the significant outcomes necessary to salvage the only home we have. It is incumbent upon each of us to make these everyday choices with both intention and foresight, for the wellbeing of our planet hangs in the balance.

# Chapter 3:
# Recycling Made Easy

As we emerge from the initial exploration of our environmental impact and the significance of seemingly minor choices, we arrive at the cradle of actionable change – recycling. The crux of sustainable living often hinges on the very systems we employ to handle our waste. In this chapter, we'll streamline the art of recycling, tailoring it to fit seamlessly into busy routines without sacrificing efficacy. Sifting through the myriad of recycling protocols need not be daunting. Instead, let's frame it as an exercise in conservation stewardship, where deciphering the cryptic symbols on packaging transforms into a simple routine, akin to taking out the trash. Stepping beyond the conventional confines of the blue bin, we don't just recycle; we re-imagine the lifecycle of our goods. This chapter lays down the foundational knowledge and introduces concise strategies to demystify recycling, ensuring that it's not just a task we do, but a conscious habit we embody in our daily quest to mend the fabric of our fragile planet.

## Navigating Recycling Codes

Our recycling journey continues with a pivotal skill that every conscientious steward of the environment must master: the deciphering of recycling codes. These enigmatic symbols found on the undersides of bottles, boxes, and various other products are the key to ensuring materials are directed to their proper recycling channels.

Recycling codes were designed to facilitate the sorting process, which is crucial for the effective recycling of materials. Much like a map guides a traveler, these codes help us navigate the occasionally convoluted landscape of recyclables. Let us delve into the intricacies of these markers and unravel their significance.

Firstly, we are often confronted by the most common emblem, the recycling triangle. Within this symbol, a number between one and seven is encased, representing different categories of plastics. Understanding these numbers is not just beneficial for recycling but also for making informed purchasing decisions. The triangle beckons us to look closer, urging us to consider the life cycle of the item in hand.

Codes "1" and "2" in the heart of the triangular arrows represent the most readily recyclable plastics: PET (Polyethylene Terephthalate) and HDPE (High-Density Polyethylene), respectively. Items bearing these codes tend to find new life fairly effortlessly within recycling programs. They remind us of the transformational power of responsible waste management, where water bottles can eventually don the guise of park benches or playground equipment.

In the realm of plastics coded "3" to "7," the path becomes more complex. PVC, LDPE, PP, and other less commonly recycled plastics may require specialized facilities to process them. A keen eye and local knowledge become assets here, ensuring these materials don't end up clogging the arteries of our ecosystems.

Understanding the implications of these codes also involves recognizing that recycling isn't always synonymous with sustainability. For instance, the number "6," which denotes Polystyrene, can be recycled, yet it's often more feasible to limit its use due to the difficulty and expense involved in its processing.

Moving beyond plastics, we encounter codes on glass, metal, and paper, each signifying a different composition or treatment. These codes are often more straightforward, allowing glass bottles, aluminum cans, and paperboard to be reincarnated with relative ease, provided they are not contaminated by residues that diminish their recyclability.

But understanding codes isn't enough; action is the true catalyst for change. It's paramount to become acquainted with your local recycling program, as not all facilities are equipped to handle every code. They might welcome number "1" and "2" plastics with open arms but shake their heads at number "7" due to the melting pot of polymers it represents.

The act of sorting materials by their codes before they reach the recycling facility can play a significant role. Stepping into the sorting process alleviates some burdens from the facilities and increases the likelihood that these materials won't be discarded due to contamination or misidentification.

We also find that some codes, like "3," seldom receive the recycling treatment due to their toxic nature when processed. This knowledge must galvanize us toward alternatives and avoidance rather than reliance on unlikely recycling outcomes.

When encountering obscure or composite materials that defy easy classification, an eco-conscious consumer must reach out to local facilities for guidance. There may be take-back programs or specialized drop-offs designed specifically for these wild cards of the recycling code game.

At this juncture, we approach the translation of theory into practice. Practicing the habit of checking and sorting by code can become second nature, a small but resolute step towards the betterment of our planet. The true environmental steward becomes a scholar of this numeric language, a translator for the good of nature.

It is this intersection of knowledge and practice, foresight, and action that molds the path to a sustainable future. As we aspire to leave behind a flourishing planet, the understanding and application of these simple numeric guidelines — these recycling codes — become small but pivotal pivots upon which the balance of ecological integrity tilts.

In the subsequent section, we eschew the strict boundaries of bins and delve into the imaginative realm of recycling, exploring creative recycling ideas that circumvent conventional methods. But the foundation remains the same—an intimate understanding of the materials we seek to reclaim.

With this nuanced grasp of recycling codes under our belt, we can stride forward with the confidence that our daily decisions are steered towards environmental benefit, contributing our individual strokes to the grand mosaic of planetary restoration.

## Beyond the Bin: Creative Recycling Ideas

As we navigate the landscape of recycling, it's essential to think outside the traditional parameters of the blue bin. While responsible disposal is critical, the creative reuse and repurposing of materials offer an innovative approach to lowering waste generation. Traditional recycling tends to focus on the familiar cycle of collecting, processing, and remaking; however, our imagination can steer us toward inventive alternatives that challenge the status quo of consumption and disposal.

The path towards sustainability necessitates embracing the understated art of upcycling, which transforms waste materials into new products with greater utility and aesthetic value. It's a flourishing domain where old T-shirts find second lives as tote bags and where discarded jars become chic lighting fixtures. Upcycling honors the energy and resources that went into the production of these items, bestowing upon them longevity that far surpasses their intended obsolescence.

In the spirit of redefining waste, one can look at old furniture not as items to be discarded, but as canvases for personal expression and creativity. Refreshing a worn-out chair or frayed dresser with a fresh coat of eco-friendly paint can infuse a room with new vibrancy, while simultaneously diverting potential landfill clutter. By learning some basic refurbishing techniques, we can single-handedly lessen the flow of bulky items to our overflowing waste management systems.

Let's also consider the potential of electronics, which are often updated and replaced at an alarming rate in our tech-thirsty society. Instead of consigning outdated gadgets to the e-waste pile, they can be repurposed. Old smartphones, for example, can be transformed into security cameras or gaming devices for children, extending their functional lifespan and delaying their date with the recycling facility.

Echoing the axiom that one man's trash is another's treasure, the trade and donation of items no longer wanted create a circular loop of reuse. Websites and local community boards are teeming with opportunities to pass on items that no longer spark joy in our lives, but may be precisely what someone else has been searching for. In this way, we not only recycle but also foster a sense of community through shared resources.

Fusing creativity with environmental stewardship, artists and craftspeople the world over use recycled materials to produce stunning artworks and practical goods. This movement not only supports the recycling industry but also shines a light on the versatility and inherent beauty of materials we typically discard without a second thought.

In urban settings, creative recycling can manifest in the form of community gardens that use old tires as planters or create functional compost bins from recycled wood pallets. By viewing the urban environment as a living ecosystem, we can use creative recycling to enhance the quality of our shared spaces while reducing waste.

Cultivating our resourcefulness, programs such as community 'fix-it' workshops encourage people to repair rather than replace. By learning how to mend a broken appliance or stitch up a tear in a favorite jacket, we empower ourselves to decrease our waste footprint — and who knows, you may just uncover a hidden talent for repairing and reviving items you once considered beyond salvation.

Adopting a philosophy where resourcefulness reigns, we can host swap meets where community members exchange their unwanted goods, from clothes to toys to books. Engaging in these exchanges not only fosters a sense of community but underscores the importance of valuing what we have and sharing it with others. It's a small but profound step towards a circular economy that champions reuse over disposal.

Achieving the reduced impact on landfills through recycling is not merely about sorting and disposing but also imagining the potential lifespans of materials. Local schools and institutions can act as a tableau for this change, integrating recycled materials into their curricula and infrastructure, thereby educating and inspiring the next generation about the possibilities of sustainable living.

Moreover, gardeners can harness the potential of recycled materials in their pursuit of beauty and yield. With ingenuity, old bathtubs can grow into raised garden beds, and cracked ceramics can gain new purpose as whimsical garden mosaic paths. Here, creative recycling marries aesthetics with ecology, crafting a functional yet captivating outdoor realm.

One could even argue that culinary pursuits offer a domain ripe for recycled innovation. Glass containers no longer limited to storing preserves can find revival as vessels for homemade candles, while wine corks can be repurposed as garden markers or crafted into bulletin boards. The intersection of culinary art and recycling beholds an untapped wellspring of possibilities, waiting to enrich our homes with both flavor and environmental mindfulness.

In the fashion industry, designers are weaving sustainability into their fabric choices by creating new collections from recycled materials. By doing so, they are challenging the norms of an industry often criticized for its wastefulness and sparking a trend where clothes consumption can be both stylish and sustainable.

Encouragingly, communities worldwide are discovering the value in salvaged building materials. From reclaimed wood beams adding rustic charm to modern homes to using crushed recycled glass in countertops, the built environment is an ever-expanding canvas for resourceful and environmentally conscious construction.

Ultimately, creative recycling demands that we look at our world through a lens of potential, seeing not what is, but what could be. As it is etched in our collective responsibility, we have the power to transform our habits and habitats. By boldly reimagining the purpose of objects that surround us, we affirm our commitment to preserving the planet for future generations. The effort to reduce, reuse, and recycle evolves into an inspiring journey of innovation — an essential narrative in the larger story of securing a viable and vibrant Earth for all its inhabitants.

# Chapter 4:
# The Magic of Composting

In the natural world, the cycle of decay and rebirth is constant, a testament to the earth's own regenerative systems. With a small effort and mindfulness, we too can harness this powerful cycle through the magic of composting. Whilst the previous chapters have fortified our understanding and approach to recycling, composting opens yet a different dimension to waste transformation. This eco-friendly process not only transforms kitchen scraps and yard waste into rich, nutrient-dense soil, but also significantly slashes landfill contributions, methane emissions, and the need for chemical fertilizers. Composting not only epitomizes the concept of turning waste into wealth, but it also represents a pivotal activity in the global effort to nourish our earth. Through the simple act of composting, we participate in nature's intricate ballet of decomposition and regeneration, fostering a healthier soil ecosystem which can sustain plant life and anchor the intricate web of our natural environment. Our dive into composting has far-reaching impacts, from revitalizing our gardens to grounding our commitment to the preservation of our planet.

## Kitchen Scraps to Garden Treasures

As we peel back the layers of sustainable living and explore the alchemy of turning everyday waste into a valuable resource, we find ourselves standing at the heart of a quiet revolution—a revolution that starts in our kitchens and ends in our gardens. The transformation of kitchen scraps into garden treasures through composting is not just an act of recycling; it's an affirmation of life's regenerative power.

Every banana peel, every coffee ground, and every wilted leaf of lettuce carries with it the potential for rebirth. Instead of dispatching these materials into the abyss of a landfill, where they release harmful methane gas as they decompose anaerobically, we have within our means the ability to craft a rich, life-giving elixir for our soil. Composting is that elegant process where waste not only loses its negative connotation but becomes an asset of immeasurable value to our gardens and the environment at large.

The kitchen is the origin of a myriad of compostable materials. While we must be selective—avoiding the inclusion of meat scraps, dairy, or oils which can attract pests and unbalance our compost's chemistry—the bulk of our daily vegetable scraps, fruit peelings, eggshells, and even paper towels are eagerly accepted by the compost bin. This act is as straightforward as setting aside these items, diverting them from the trash, and reintroducing them to the earth from whence they came.

But how do these scraps become the sought-after "black gold" that gardeners covet? The answer lies within the microscopic ecosystem that thrives within every compost heap. Here, a battalion of bacteria, fungi, and other decomposers play a pivotal role. They break down organic matter, recycle nutrients, and in doing so, create a nourishing humus that breathes life back into depleted soils.

For those new to composting, the practice may seem daunting, encumbered by ratios of 'greens' to 'browns' and concerns over odors and pests. But fear not, for the essence of composting dwells in simplicity. It requires little more than the layering of wet scraps with drier, carbon-rich materials like leaves or shredded newspaper—a repeatable process that gradually builds into a fertile repository.

Maintaining a compost pile is akin to tending a garden: it asks for a balance of attention and patience. Compost requires aeration, a bit like stirring a hearty stew, to provide the oxygen that aerobic bacteria need to do their work efficiently. Occasionally adding water keeps the pile moist, a vital factor in sustaining the decomposition process. With these small, but consistent acts of care, your scraps will gracefully transition into a nutrient-dense amendment for soil.

One may even witness the rise in temperature within the pile as microbial activity intensifies, a testament to the transformative power at play. However, it's crucial to remember that a successful compost pile is an inclusive habitat, offering sanctuary to larger organisms like worms and beetles, considered the champions of organic breakdown.

The benefits of this kitchen to garden loop are manifold. By adding compost to our gardens, we not only provide our plants with essential nutrients but also improve soil structure, water retention, and introduce beneficial microorganisms which contribute to a naturally resilient garden ecosystem.

Yet the influence of composting extends beyond the boundaries of our backyards. It's an intimate engagement with the natural cycle of life, death, and rebirth that provides a stark counterpoint to the disposable culture that has contributed to ecological decay. In composting, we step back into symbiosis with the planet. We're reminded that what we cast aside isn't just waste, but an offering to the circle of life.

Many might question the scale of impact that composting at home can have in the face of global environmental challenges. However, it's crucial to recognize that each compost heap diminishes the strain on our landfills, reduces greenhouse gas emissions, and conserves water—all while empowering individuals with a direct path to environmental stewardship.

Composting also has an educational aspect, particularly for young minds. It demonstrates the cycle of organic life in a tangible way, teaching principles of ecology, biology, and responsible waste management—all essential for a generation that will inherit the task of nurturing our planet.

Patience is a virtue in composting, as the transformation from scraps to soil conditioner isn't immediate. It embodies the principle of delayed gratification—a concept at odds with the 'instant' society we've become. Yet, the reward for such patience is sweet: rich, fertile soil that will nourish the foods we eat and the flowers we admire for seasons to come.

Finally, it's a practice that extends an open invitation to all willing to contribute to a greener future. It asks little of us, just a redirection of what we already have. There's a quaint poetry in imagining the peels from our morning's orange, given time, could bloom into the ripe tomatoes or crisp lettuce of tomorrow. Such is the lowly, yet profound power of composting—a cycle that turns what was once seen as waste into a bountiful treasure for our gardens and a hopeful gesture for our world.

In this way, composting is not just a chapter in the story of ecological redemption, it's a blueprint for a more thoughtful interaction with our environment. As we deposit our kitchen scraps into the compost bin, we invest in our planet's future. The transformation into garden treasure is slow but sure, signaling a change in our relationship with the Earth—a change that speaks of respect, renewal, and ultimately, hope.

As the final thought lingers, it's worth savoring the quiet significance of composting. Not merely a means to an end, but rather an experience that brings us closer to the intricate and precious balance of life. And in this small, humbling act of recycling our scraps, we find resonance with a far greater narrative—one of stewardship, legacy, and the kind of magic that roots as deeply in our hearts as it does in our gardens.

## Community Composting: Getting Involved Locally

In our journey to reconnect with the earth and align our lives with the rhythmic cycles of nature, we find an often-overlooked gem: composting. Harnessing the decay process to return nutrients to the soil is not just a practice for individual households; it's a movement that's gaining traction within communities across the globe. Let's delve into the grassroots efforts that epitomize community composting and explore how you can become an integral part of this environmental renaissance.

Community composting is where individuals come together to share the responsibilities and rewards of composting organic waste. These localized efforts provide an avenue to reduce landfill waste, foster soil fertility, and unite neighbors in a common goal—a healthier planet.

The first step to involvement often starts with a simple act: educating oneself about the dynamics of community composting. Many cities and towns now offer composting programs, which often include workshops and resources to help residents understand the process and benefits of community-scale composting.

Once you're acquainted with the basics, seek out or initiate a composting program in your area. This could be an established community garden that accepts compostable waste or a dedicated composting site managed by local environmental groups. Some neighborhoods even operate through a collection service, akin to traditional recycling programs, ensuring that even the busiest individuals can contribute.

Participation doesn't require expert knowledge in compost science. Volunteers at community composting sites can assist in various tasks, from turning compost piles to educating new members. Every hand contributes to the workload, and the act of volunteering can be both enlightening and deeply fulfilling.

Funding is often a concern for community composting initiatives. Grants and local government support can be instrumental, but don't overlook the power of crowdfunding and community-driven fundraisers. After all, sustainability isn't just an environmental concept, it also pertains to the viability of these valuable programs.

To make community composting a success, public engagement is crucial. Regular community meetings and open days can create a welcoming environment for all residents. By offering workshops and open tours, these events serve to demystify composting and show its tangible benefits to the community.

Collaboration extends beyond individuals. Establishing partnerships with local businesses, schools, and restaurants to divert their organic waste to the community composting program can have a dramatic impact on the volume of waste turned into valuable compost.

Transparency and communication are key components of an effective community composting program. Regular updates about the program's progress, stories of success, and the impact assessment on waste reduction can keep the community informed and engaged, fostering a strong sense of collective achievement.

Maintaining momentum can be a challenge, but the shared leadership model in which responsibilities are distributed among members encourages broader participation and investment in the project's success. This approach can empower individuals and prevent burnout among organizers.

As you contribute to the communal pile, you'll appreciate the symbiotic relationship between waste and renewal. Composting at this scale illustrates the circular economy in action—a concept that is vital for the longevity of our resources and ecosystems.

Monitoring and evaluating the community composting program are critical for identifying areas for improvement. Regularly analyzing the quality of the compost produced, the efficiency of the composting process, and the program's environmental impact leads to informed decisions and the evolution of best practices.

An essential part of community composting is celebrating the milestones reached. Whether it's the first successful batch of compost or the hundredth ton of waste diverted from landfills, these achievements validate the efforts of all involved and inspire continued dedication to environmental stewardship.

Community composting goes beyond dealing with waste. It's a cultural shift towards a sustainable coexistence with the planet. By involving yourself in local composting efforts, you become a catalyst for change, influencing others and embedding ecological consciousness into the fabric of your community.

So, as we move forward on this shared path to preserve the fragility of our earth, let us recognize composting's role as a powerful agent of transformation. It's not just about returning nutrients to the soil; it's about nurturing a connected community that values every aspect of our natural world. By throwing your organic scraps into the community compost, you're laying the groundwork for regeneration. Thus, a cycle of life and prosperity for the earth is sustained—one handful of compost at a time.

# Chapter 5:
# Reducing Household Waste

As we transition from the richness of compost to the broader scope of household refuse, it's crucial to highlight that every item we choose not to waste is a step towards the regeneration of our strained ecosystems. In reducing household waste, the quest isn't merely to discard less; it is a conscious, deliberate journey to halt the tide of refuse at its source. We must scrutinize the lifecycle of everyday items, from production to disposal, and acknowledge our pivotal role within this cycle. Reducing waste calls for an introspective evaluation of consumption habits coupled with a steadfast resolve. By doing so, we can interrupt the otherwise relentless stream of materials that burden landfills and incinerators. Whether it's avoiding disposable items that plague our pantries or seeking out sustainable cleaning products, the strategies we employ reverberate through the intricacies of environmental wellbeing. The pathway to minimal waste isn't laced with deprivation but rather enriched with innovation and a sense of responsibility towards the only home we have.

## Minimizing Single-Use Products

In our earnest journey toward reducing household waste, a critical area to address is the ubiquitous presence of single-use products. These disposable items, though convenient, represent a monumental source of waste, contributing to overflowing landfills and ocean pollution. Our ability to minimize our reliance on such products can have a profound effect on the environment, reducing the strain we impose on our planet's precious resources.

The convenience of single-use items is overshadowed by their environmental impacts. Single-use plastics, such as shopping bags, water bottles, straws, and utensils, are typically used only once before they end up discarded. This cycle of short-term use and long-term pollution can be interrupted by adopting more sustainable practices within our households. The transition involves rethinking our daily habits, favoring reusable alternatives, and understanding the longevity and lifecycle of the products we consume.

To begin with, the most direct approach to minimize single-use products is to outright avoid them. Opt for reusable shopping bags instead of the plastic or paper options provided at stores. Keep a cloth tote or a foldable bag with you for unexpected purchases to circumvent the need for single-use bags. Similarly, investing in a durable water bottle eliminates the need for purchasing bottled water. Stainless steel, glass, and BPA-free plastic options are readily available, allowing not just a reduction in waste but often an improvement in the quality of the water we drink.

Moreover, the food industry is notorious for its reliance on single-use packaging. The next time you order takeout or a beverage from a cafe, consider providing your own containers or mugs. It's a small gesture that, when collectively practiced, can lead to a substantial decrease in waste. In many places, businesses are beginning to reward such actions with discounts, acknowledging the role customers play in sustainability efforts.

At home, re-evaluate the use of single-use items in daily activities. Cling film, aluminum foil, and parchment paper, for instance, have reusable alternatives in the form of beeswax wraps, silicone lids, and reusable baking mats. These items not only reduce waste but are also cost-effective in the long run. Transitioning to these options requires an initial investment, but the payoff, both financially and environmentally, is significant.

Personal care also offers fertile ground for change. Disposable razors, menstrual products, and cotton swabs contribute heavily to personal waste. Consider switching to safety razors with replaceable blades, menstrual cups or cloth pads, and biodegradable cotton swabs. These products are not only less harmful to the environment but also tend to offer better experiences and longer durations of use.

In the realm of housekeeping, teach yourself to reach for a washable cloth instead of paper towels. Microfiber cloths, sponges, and mop systems designed for multiple uses can effectively replace paper products for cleaning up spills and daily household chores. With each wash and reuse, you're chipping away at the mountain of paper waste that burdens landfills.

When hosting parties or events, resist the lure of disposable tableware. Although the clean-up may seem daunting, using real dishes, cups, and silverware adds an element of respect for both your guests and the environment. Renting tableware is a viable option for large gatherings, and compostable tableware can serve as a middle ground when the real thing is not practical.

Single-use items in packaging further contribute to waste, and being selective on this front can make a difference. Buying in bulk, when possible, reduces the quantity of packaging used for individual items. Many stores now offer bulk purchases for a variety of goods, from dry foods to cleaning products, allowing consumers to fill their own reusable containers and avoid unnecessary packaging.

It must be underscored that recycling, while beneficial, is not a cure-all solution for single-use product pollution. A significant amount of plastics cannot be recycled effectively, and the process itself uses resources. The most impactful choice remains to reduce first, choosing not to bring single-use items into our homes whenever possible.

Engagement and education can also extend to our workplaces and social circles. Encourage your workplace to reduce single-use utensils and provide employees with reusable options. Discussing the importance of minimizing single-use products with friends and family can help spread awareness and change consumption patterns within your community.

Look out for products with certifications indicating biodegradability or that they've been sustainably sourced. These certifications, while sometimes more expensive, reveal a commitment to environmental responsibility, often ensuring that products can break down naturally or are produced with minimal harm to the environment.

In essence, minimizing single-use products is about re-tooling our lifestyle habits for sustainability. It requires endeavor and patience, but the collective benefits are invaluable. Each reusable bottle, each cloth bag, each sustainable swap builds towards a more harmonious relationship with our environment.

Awareness of the impacts of single-use products and the determination to make changes in our daily consumption patterns constitute some of the most powerful actions we can take in the fight to save our planet. True transformation is seeded in the understanding that every choice — every item we refuse, reduce, or reuse — can mend the rift between our modern way of life and the health of our ecosystems.

As our hands wield the power to make the necessary changes, let us embrace the notion that the path to a sustainable future is paved with the decisions we make today. Minimizing single-use products isn't merely an act of conservation; it's a definitive statement about the kind of world we wish to inhabit and bequeath to generations to come.

## Eco-Friendly Cleaning Alternatives

In the vein of minimizing household waste and furthering our commitment to the environment, let's delve into eco-friendly cleaning alternatives. The everyday cleaning products and methods we employ play a pivotal role in both our homes' purity and the planet's health.

The traditional cleaning aisle is a dazzling display of chemical concoctions promising germ-free surfaces and sparkling cleanliness. However, many of these cleaners contain hazardous substances that can contaminate waterways, harm wildlife, and even adversely affect our own well-being.

One foundational step towards reducing this impact is implementing simple, eco-friendly cleaning strategies. Replacing chemical-laden solutions with natural cleaners is not only better for the Earth but also for the air quality within our homes.

**Vinegar**, for instance, is a versatile, natural cleaning agent that can tackle everything from window grime to mineral deposits. Its acidic nature cuts through grease and bacteria, leaving behind a clean, albeit temporarily pungent, freshness.

*Baking soda* is another household staple that can be repurposed as a cleaning powerhouse. Its mild abrasive texture is ideal for scrubbing away tough stains without scratching surfaces, while its deodorizing properties help to neutralize unwanted odors.

When paired together, vinegar and baking soda can even unclog drains without the need for harsh commercial drain openers. The bubbling reaction dislodges blockages, providing an environmentally safe solution to a common household issue.

Citrus peels, steeped in vinegar, create an effective and fragrant all-purpose cleaner. The citrus oils break down grease, and the vinegar takes care of bacteria and germs, leaving behind a refreshing scent once the initial vinegar smell dissipates.

Castile soap, a plant-based product, is gentle yet effective for a myriad of uses, from mopping floors to personal hygiene. It's biodegradable, safe for the Earth, and concentrated, reducing the need for large, bulky containers.

Essential oils are not just for aromatherapy; they can be potent allies in the fight against bacteria and viruses. Adding oils like tea tree, lavender, or eucalyptus to homemade cleaning mixes can enhance their antimicrobial properties.

For those daunting chores that seem to call for the brute force of bleach, consider using hydrogen peroxide as a safer alternative. It has similar whitening and disinfecting capabilities without the same level of toxicity or risk to the environment.

Switching to **microfiber cloths** or cleaning with old t-shirts can reduce the use of disposable products like paper towels. These reusable options can be laundered and employed repeatedly, saving trees and landfill space.

In place of scouring pads, consider using natural abrasives like salt or even walnut shells. These alternatives are effective in scrubbing off grime and are completely biodegradable.

Steam cleaning is a powerful, chemical-free method capable of sanitizing surfaces, floors, and even upholstery. The high heat of steam kills bacteria and mites and only requires water, making it an excellent choice for those eliminating chemicals from their cleaning routine entirely.

Investing in a high-quality **HEPA vacuum** cleaner is advantageous for capturing allergens and fine particles without releasing them back into the home. This contributes to better indoor air quality and requires fewer resources over time compared to disposables like vacuum bags.

When you require the convenience of ready-to-use products, seeking out brands that emphasize eco-friendly practices is crucial. Look for companies that use sustainable packaging, biodegradable ingredients, and have a demonstrated commitment to environmental stewardship.

Lastly, adopting an overall minimalist approach to cleaning can make a substantial difference. Focusing on high-impact cleaning, using less product, and buying concentrates that can be diluted at home are all strategies that lead to less waste.

In implementing eco-friendly cleaning alternatives, we not only protect our immediate surroundings but also contribute positively to the broader environmental outlook. It's a simple shift, yet an impactful one, aligning with our ongoing efforts to reduce household waste for a more sustainable future.

# Chapter 6:
# Water Conservation Tactics

As we transition from reducing household waste, it's crucial to recognize the essential role water plays in our lives and the growing urgency to preserve this precious resource. In "Water Conservation Tactics," we delve into practical strategies that can be seamlessly incorporated into everyday life to reduce water consumption and waste. The chapter outlines methods to manage water use sensibly, not only for the sustainability of our planet but also for the resilience of our communities. With a focus on efficacy and simplicity, these techniques are crafted for easy adoption by anyone keen on contributing to the collective effort of water preservation. By illuminating the profound impact of mindful water usage, this chapter empowers individuals to take actionable steps towards a sustainable water future and highlights the undeniable truth that every conservation effort, no matter how seemingly small, can cumulate into a tide of change vital for our survival.

## Saving H2O in Daily Routines

Within the compendium of water conservation tactics, we find a most crucial domain: the incorporation of H2O-saving strategies into our daily routines. The onus lies not solely on industry giants or government policies; the power of the individual resonates profoundly when we all take small, persistent steps towards a sustainable future. This section delves into the practical measures one can adopt to curtail water usage within the rhythm of daily life, an effort that yields both ecological balance and a sense of personal stewardship over our shared resources.

Commence your day with mindfulness; in the realm of conserving water, the morning routine is rife with opportunity. Consider the act of brushing your teeth—a task so mundane, and yet it can have multiplying effects. Turn off the tap while brushing. This action alone can save gallons over the course of a month, should every household adhere to this simple practice.

The shower—a sanctuary of solitude and thought—can also become a bastion of conservation. By installing a low-flow showerhead, one can significantly reduce the gallons per minute used without sacrificing the comfort of water pressure. In addition, limiting showers to the necessary duration has the potential to diminish water consumption even further.

Laundry serves as another front in our effort to preserve this precious resource. By opting for full loads only, you maximize the efficiency of water use with each cycle. For those with a choice in the matter, investing in a high-efficiency washing machine can place a substantial damper on household water usage, aligning your routine with conservation goals.

The same philosophy applies to the dishwasher—running this appliance only when fully loaded avoids unnecessary cycles. For the dishes that don't quite fill the machine, consider hand-washing in a basin rather than under running water, a tactic that can control usage to a finite quantity.

When considering what keeps our gardens and plants flourishing, a shift towards water-wise landscaping can lead to remarkable savings. Drought-resistant plants and drip irrigation systems target water exactly where it's needed, minimizing waste from evaporation and runoff.

An often overlooked aspect is the quest to identify and repair leaks. A faucet dripping once per second can waste upwards of 3,000 gallons annually. A vigilant approach to plumbing can help plug these leaks, transforming potential waste into conserved resources.

And let's talk about the kitchen sink—become strategical about its use. When it's necessary to rinse fruits and vegetables, do so in a bowl of water rather than under a running faucet. This water can later be repurposed to water household plants or for cleaning purposes.

Conservation can also extend into our culinary practices. When boiling pasta or vegetables, try using less water and covering the pot with a lid to retain heat and reduce the amount of water brought to a boil. This not only saves water but also energy, a double win for environmental conscientiousness.

Iced drinks and water filtration are a staple in many homes. Rather than letting the tap run cold, fill a jug and store it in the refrigerator. Furthermore, this chilled water can be refilled into reusable bottles, reducing the need for the production of single-use plastics, thus saving on the water used in their manufacturing processes.

Monitoring the water meter can also enlighten us to our consumption patterns, allowing for targeted reduction strategies. Occasional readings provide insight into daily usage and can also alert homeowners to otherwise invisible leaks within their system.

In restrooms, installing a dual-flush or low-flow toilet constitutes a significant water-saving upgrade. For older toilets, a displacement device in the tank can reduce the volume of water used per flush—a DIY water conservation effort.

During the warmer months, water use can spike due to outdoor activities. Here, conservation can be as simple as using a pool cover to minimize evaporation or sweeping driveways and sidewalks instead of hosing them down, which not only conserves water but encourages physical activity.

Shifting our habits while cleaning can make sizable dents in water use as well. Opt for a bucket and sponge when washing your car, and choose biodegradable soaps to ensure you safeguard both water and soil from contaminants.

Finally, educating ourselves and others about the importance of water conservation solidifies the practice in our communities. Share your knowledge with neighbors and friends. Foster a culture of conservation where these daily acts become as customary as the routines themselves.

To conclude, the cumulative impact of individual efforts towards saving H2O in our daily routines can ripple out to tangible gains for our planet. It is in the micro-adjustments to our lifestyles, the embracing of small-scale changes, that we find the true power to influence the course of our ecological journey. With every drop saved, we write a new narrative—an ode to the vitality of water and the role it plays in our collective existence.

**Fixing Leaks: Every Drop Counts** As our journey through water conservation tactics continues, it's crucial to address one of the most common and often overlooked issues impacting our precious water resources: leaks. With an ear to conservation and a resolve to safeguard every drop, this chapter zeroes in on the significance of addressing household leaks.

In the quest to converse water, it's illuminating to acknowledge that even the smallest leak is not merely a household inconvenience; it's a symptom of a larger issue at play. A dripping faucet, with its incessant pitter-patter, can waste gallons of water over the course of a year. To put this into perspective, consider that a single leak can amount to the loss of a resource that is desperately needed in many parts of the world. This waste is a luxury we can no longer afford.

Commencing the leak-fixing process involves vigilance. Monthly checks around the home for any signs of leaks, including under sinks, around appliance connections, and outdoor spigots, make identifying problems swiftly a much simpler task. Being proactive not only assists in water preservation but also protects your home from potential water damage, which can escalate into costly repairs.

Don't underestimate the power of knowledge. Understanding how to replace a worn washer or apply plumbing tape can equip homeowners with the means to tackle minor leaks immediately. There are countless tutorials and guides available, making these valuable skills within reach for those who might not consider themselves particularly handy.

For problematic leaks or if you're unsure about DIY repairs, calling a professional plumber is a responsible step toward water conservation. It's an investment that not only assures the job is done correctly but also contributes to a more sustainable home and planet. These experts can reveal hidden leaks that go unnoticed, like those that might occur within walls or beneath the house foundation.

The commitment to fix leaks extends to the community level as well. Water supply systems, some of which are outdated or deteriorating, account for substantial water loss annually. Encouraging local governments to invest in water infrastructure not only ensures efficiency but also demonstrates a collective commitment to conserving this vital resource.

Beyond repairs, technology offers innovative solutions, such as smart home water monitors that detect leaks and abnormal water usage patterns. These devices provide real-time information and alerts, allowing homeowners to address leaks promptly and manage water usage judiciously.

It may seem that individual efforts to fix leaks are but a drop in the bucket when considering the global water crisis. However, if every household took responsibility for their water usage and leakage, the cumulative effect would be a drastic reduction in needless water consumption. It is through these small yet deliberate actions that significant change happens.

Remember, water conservation is not just about using less; it's about wasting less. Fixing leaks is a reflection of respect for one of our most essential natural resources. By paying attention to the little things, we are contributing to a world where clean water is cherished and preserved—for our generation and those to follow.

In combining hands-on action with a consciousness of consumption, the mantra every drop counts becomes our guiding principle. As we forge ahead towards an era that holds promise for a more sustainable balance with Earth's resources, let us not ignore the silent plea of a leaky faucet, for in every unwanted drip, there lies the potential to save both water and our planet.

# Chapter 7:
# Lowering Your Carbon Footprint

As we journey deeper into the quest for a sustainable existence, Chapter 7 focuses on actionable strategies for *Lowering Your Carbon Footprint*. Each choice we make, from how we commute to the items we consume, casts a shadow on the environment. Embarking on the path of green transportation is more than replacing car keys with bicycle helmets; it embodies a commitment to tread lightly on the earth. This chapter does not simply prescribe but elucidates the ecological merit of each stride and pedal in creating a greener future. We'll delve into the intricacies that define a low-carbon lifestyle where the subtleties of daily living, be it the route we take to work or the energy we rely on to power our lives, add up to a profound reduction in greenhouse gas emissions. Understanding the gravitas of our carbon footprint is pivotal, for in its depth lies the blueprint to a resilient planet. We'll explore, dissect, and reconstruct our habits in this section, framing a life that both gratifies our needs and safeguards our world.

## Green Transportation for a Greener Future

As we pivot from discussions on household waste and water conservation, it's time to cast our gaze on green transportation—a vital component of lowering our carbon footprint. With each turn of an engine, we edge imperceptibly closer to irreversible climate change. Yet, transportation is an arena teeming with sustainable promise, an opportunity to make an earnest difference on both a personal and collective level.

Consider the ramifications of our ubiquitous car culture. It's not just the carbon dioxide emissions; it's also particulate matter, nitrogen oxides, and other pollutants that tarnish our air, endanger our health, and exacerbate global warming. Cars are the stalwarts of convenience, but their environmental costs are untenable. Transitioning to green transportation isn't just advisable; it is imperative for our planet's health.

Electric vehicles (EVs) are rapidly becoming more accessible, portending a future where our commutes are not detrimental to Earth's well-being. With zero tailpipe emissions, EVs offer a beacon of hope. Nevertheless, the true environmental impact of electric vehicles spans beyond emissions, forging into the territory of sustainable battery production and responsible sourcing of materials.

Public transportation is another cornerstone of green living. By opting for buses, trains, or subways, we not only decrease our personal carbon output but also support infrastructure that can scale and eventually offset a significant portion of vehicular emissions. Cities around the globe are retrofocusing their efforts to enhance public transit connectivity and efficiency, making it a more appealing option for commuters.

The allure of car sharing and ride-hailing services lies in their potential to reduce the need for personal vehicle ownership. By sharing rides, we not only economize on costs but also on the carbon cost of manufacturing and maintaining multiple vehicles. Moreover, when these services integrate EVs into their fleets, the benefits multiply.

Let us not underestimate the potency of biking and walking, discussed in more detail in the following section. These modes of transport engender numerous benefits: decreased emissions, reduced traffic congestion, improved public health and well-being, and more liveable urban environments.

Investing in micro-mobility options such as scooters and e-bikes is another measure to foster a greener future. These conveyances can effectively bridge the "last mile" gap, providing a sustainable option for the short distances that are too long to walk but wastefully short for car travel.

Telecommuting, once a luxury, has been thrust to the forefront by recent global circumstances. The resultant decrease in daily commuting has been a windfall for emissions reduction. Encouraging flexible work arrangements where feasible can continue this positive trend.

The development of low-impact fuels, like biofuels and hydrogen, promises a transition to greener aviation and shipping industries. Although not without their own challenges, these alternatives show potential to mitigate the hefty carbon footprint of air and sea travel.

Infrastructure facilitates or frustrates our best green intentions. Investment in sustainable urban planning, including dedicated cycling lanes and pedestrian zones, can dramatically alter the fabric of our transportation habits, incentivizing green choices.

Equity in transportation is inextricably linked to environmental justice. Ensuring that green transportation options are available to individuals across different economic spectrums is critical. Accessible, affordable, and sustainable transportation options need to be a universal priority.

Policy initiatives often drive significant change. By advocating for policies that promote green transportation—such as tax incentives for EVs, funding for public transit, and research into alternative fuels—we support a structural shift towards sustainability.

Education is crucial for driving change. Many people remain unaware of the environmental impact our transport choices exert. Increasing awareness of the options available and their associated benefits can steer consumer and political action towards a greener future.

Finally, individual action interlocks with collective progress. Aligning our personal transportation choices with our environmental values denotes an indispensable step toward a sustainable future. The cumulative effect of millions making greener transport choices can turn the tide, contributing to a cleaner, healthier planet.

In conclusion, the path towards green transportation is multifaceted, ranging from innovations in technology to changes in cultural norms. Each stride, whether it's swapping a gas-powered car for an EV or simply choosing to bike to work, is a crucial component in this crucial journey. As we steer away from reliance on fossil fuels, we navigate towards a responsible, thriving coexistence with our environment—a future where humanity moves in harmony with the Earth's delicate balance.

**The Benefits of Biking and Walking** as modes of transportation are not merely confined to personal well-being; they inherently contribute to environmental conservation and play a vital role in mitigating climate change. Both activities serve as keystones in the archway leading to a sustainable future, simultaneously improving public health and reducing carbon emissions.

When individuals choose to cycle or walk, even for short distances, there are immediate reductions in air pollutants and greenhouse gases. Cars, which are among the most significant contributors to urban emissions, often sit idle in traffic, especially during rush hours, emitting exhaust even when not actively traveling. Biking and walking, on the other hand, produce zero emissions, leading directly to cleaner air quality in cities and neighborhoods.

The shift away from vehicular travel to human-powered transportation can also lead to substantial energy savings. The calories burned and the energy expended by walking and cycling come from renewable human energy, generated from the food we consume. Contrastingly, vehicles require non-renewable fossil fuels, which contribute to resource depletion and environmental degradation.

Furthermore, the infrastructure required for bikes and pedestrians is significantly less invasive and damaging to natural landscapes than that which is required for motorized vehicles. More biking paths and walking trails can mean less deforestation and ecosystem disruption, generating spaces that foster biodiversity alongside human health and connectivity.

Audible in the symphony of benefits is the resulting reduction of noise pollution. Cities besieged by the constant hum of traffic find solace in the soft whispers of bicycle chains and the rhythmic beat of footsteps. This quiet revolution can improve urban living conditions and reduce stress-related illnesses.

Biking and walking also promote better land use by reducing the necessity for sprawling parking lots and multi-lane roads that consume vast tracts of land. In their stead, communities can be designed or restructured with green spaces and corridors that encourage biodiversity, recreation, and social cohesion.

The impact on the urban heat island effect is not to be overlooked. Without the incessant heat from car engines and the reduction in asphalt coverage required for roads and parking spaces, cities can better manage their temperature levels. The increased vegetation from expanded green spaces also aids in cooling urban areas and contributes to climate change mitigation strategies.

There exists an economic dimension to consider as well. The lessened demand for oil and the associated political and environmental costs of drilling and transportation are significant. People who regularly bike or walk often experience savings on fuel costs, vehicle maintenance, and parking fees, not to mention the health benefits that may lead to lowered healthcare expenses over time.

This section would be remiss without acknowledging the potential for improved mental health and community engagement through these modes of transportation. Interacting with one's environment at a slower pace allows for a more intimate connection with nature and the community. It can foster a sense of belonging and purpose as individuals take direct, daily action to protect the planet they inhabit.

To surmise, the reverberations of choosing to bike and walk over the convenience of personal vehicles are wide-ranging and deeply interconnected with the broader environmental tapestry. As cities evolve and individuals become more cognizant of their choices' impact, embracing these sustainable means of transportation becomes not only beneficial but essential in our effort to preserve ecosystems and ensure a habitable planet for future generations.

# Chapter 8:
# Energy Efficiency at Home

In the preceding chapters, we've approached eco-conscious living from several angles, underlining the significance of individual action. Transitioning fluidly into the realm of energy efficiency, this chapter shall bring into focus strategies and practices to curtail domestic energy consumption, aiming not only to trim down utility bills but also to lessen the carbon emissions choking our planet. As we move indoors, let us consider the home not just as a sanctuary, but as a pivotal frontline in the battle against ecological decline. We'll explore how optimizing our living spaces and consciously selecting appliances can elevate our homes into models of sustainability. Note that our emphasis here isn't on exhaustive lists or technical jargon but on fostering an intuitive sense of energy stewardship that seamlessly integrates into daily routines. Whether it be the whisper of LED lights illuminating our evenings or the soft hum of an ENERGY STAR-rated refrigerator, the resonance of reduced energy usage is a testament to our commitment to Mother Earth's future.

## Cutting Electricity Costs and Carbon Emissions

In the quest for a more sustainable future, homes across the globe are becoming battlegrounds against energy waste and greenhouse gas emissions. The impact of our domestic living extends far beyond the boundary of our property lines, influencing the global narrative on climate change and resource stewardship.

One of the most straightforward strategies for homeowners is to scrutinize their energy consumption diligently. By dissecting our energy bills and understanding where we can make adjustments, we are taking the first step toward substantial change. The goal is transparent: slash energy costs and carbon emissions, creating homes that are not only more economical to run but also kinder to our precious environment.

Inadequate insulation and older windows are silent culprits of energy waste. Upgrading to high-efficiency windows and bolstering insulation can trap warmth during winter and keep homes cool in summer, reducing the need for constant heating and air conditioning. This investment is an enduring solution that pays dividends for both your wallet and the atmosphere.

Switching to LED light bulbs is another actionable measure we can all implement with relative ease. These bulbs last markedly longer and consume considerably less electricity than their incandescent predecessors. With lighting accounting for a notable percentage of home energy use, the leap to LED is a bright idea for conserving power and mitigating emissions.

The phantom draw of electricity by gadgets and appliances left on standby mode can add up, little by little, to a significant and needless energy drain. By habitually unplugging devices when not in use or employing smart power strips that halt energy flow to idle electronics, households can effortlessly curtail the insidious energy bleed.

The use of programmable thermostats is an effective way to automate energy savings. These devices can adjust your home's temperature according to your schedule, ensuring comfort while you're present and energy conservation when you're away. With less energy spent on unnecessary heating and cooling, your carbon footprint can shrink substantially.

Homeowners should not overlook the advantages of harnessing renewable energy sources. Systems like solar panels may entail an initial investment, but the returns are significant — reducing reliance on fossil fuels and providing renewable power that curtails greenhouse gas emissions. What's more, many regions offer incentives or rebates for renewable energy installations.

Water heating accounts for a considerable slice of household energy consumption. Transitioning to an energy-efficient water heater, or better yet, a solar water heating system, can effectually cut both energy use and utility expenses. Moreover, minimal adjustments like reducing water heater temperatures can yield surprising savings.

Large appliances such as refrigerators, washing machines, and dryers are typically heavy users of electricity. Investing in ENERGY STAR-rated appliances when replacements are needed ensures that your household operations are as energy efficient as possible. Though the initial cost may be higher, the long-term savings — both monetarily and environmentally — are substantial.

Maintaining and cleaning appliances regularly can also lead to energy savings. Simple actions like replacing filters in air conditioners and dryers improve efficiency and extend the lifespan of these machines. Proper maintenance not only prevents energy leakage but also decreases the frequency of costly replacements.

While considering reductions in energy use, we mustn't ignore the small daily habits that accumulate over time. Taking shorter showers, air-drying laundry, and cooking with lids on pots are micro-actions that contribute to the macro goal of energy conservation. These habits, once embedded into daily life, can collectively result in notable energy savings.

Community energy initiatives and green tariffs from electricity providers can also shape our approach to energy consumption. By supporting and participating in such programs, homeowners can ensure their energy is sourced from renewable and low-carbon options, fostering an energy-economical community ethos.

Energy audits present a professional way of identifying where a home is losing energy and where improvements can be made. Engaging a certified energy rater can provide bespoke solutions tailored to your home's unique needs, charting a course for energy and cost reduction while boosting home comfort.

Smart home technology, with its array of sensors and connected devices, allows for impressive oversight and control over home energy usage. Armed with data and the capacity to make adjustments remotely, residents can finely tune their energy consumption, trimming down on waste as never before.

Each action, from the smallest to the most grandiose, is a stitch in the fabric of a more sustainable future. Homes are not just shelters but are part of the ecosystem that is our planet. By continually committing to cutting electricity costs and carbon emissions, we protect our homesteads and contribute to the healing of Mother Earth.

**Choosing Energy-Saving Appliances** In our ongoing effort to reduce our carbon footprints, turning attention toward the energy consumption of household appliances is a critical step. After all, each appliance contributes to the total energy demand of a household, and by extension impacts the climate crisis at hand.

When contemplating energy-saving appliances, it's essential to understand the concept of 'energy efficiency.' Simply put, this refers to using less energy to perform the same task. The benefits of choosing energy-efficient appliances are twofold: they reduce household energy costs and contribute to significant environmental protection by curbing unnecessary energy consumption and greenhouse gas emissions.

To guide consumers, the Environmental Protection Agency (EPA) has created the ENERGY STAR program. Appliances bearing the ENERGY STAR label meet strict energy efficiency guidelines set by the EPA and the Department of Energy (DOE). By opting for these certified products, one can be assured they are purchasing some of the most efficient devices available, which can lead to substantial savings over the appliance's lifespan.

When in the market for new appliances, sizing is another crucial consideration. It isn't just about fitting into a designated space in your home, but also ensuring that the appliance's capacity is appropriate for your needs. Over-sized air conditioners, heaters, refrigerators, or even laundry machines will consume more energy than necessary, leading to wasted electricity and higher bills.

Moreover, modern technology and innovation have introduced 'smart' appliances, equipped with sophisticated features designed to save energy. These devices can be programmed to operate at non-peak hours, further reducing the strain on the power grid and your wallet. Additionally, some smart appliances are equipped with sensors to optimize their operation, such as refrigerators that adjust cooling based on the amount of content or washing machines that assess the load to determine the essential amount of water.

Another aspect to consider is the long-term cost of owning an appliance. While energy-saving appliances may sometimes carry a higher initial price tag, the ongoing operation costs are often lower. Before making a purchase, calculate the total cost of ownership, which includes purchase price, operational costs, and expected lifespan. This comprehensive evaluation better represents the true cost and savings associated with energy-efficient options.

It's also wise to research and take advantage of any rebates, incentives, or tax credits offered for purchasing energy-efficient appliances. Many government programs are designed to encourage the transition to more sustainable consumer behavior.

Maintenance plays a critical role in the overall efficiency of your appliances. Even the most energy-efficient appliance can waste energy if not properly looked after. Regularly cleaning, servicing, and repairing appliances extends their life and ensures that they run at peak efficiency.

In conclusion, the decision to invest in energy-saving appliances is an investment in the future of our planet. Initiating changes in purchasing habits and home appliance usage not only cuts down on personal energy bills but also contributes to the global effort of reducing the strain on our planet's resources. The cumulative effect of these individual decisions can't be overstated; together, they possess the potential to alter the trajectory toward a more sustainable world.

As the preceding chapters have established, our individual choices do indeed have power. As we continue to explore ways to reduce our carbon footprint in subsequent chapters, let us carry with us the understanding that each action, each decision to choose a sustainable alternative, is a vital strand in the web of change we are collectively weaving.

# Chapter 9:
# Mindful Eating for the Planet

Transitioning from the comfort of familiar energy solutions to the dining table, we confront another significant influence on our planet's health—our diets. The act of eating, often mindless and steeped in routine, holds a profound potential to either perpetuate environmental harm or foster regeneration. Amindful approach to consumption proves pivotal; it's the convergence of knowledge, intention, and action that can reshape our food systems. By making conscious choices, such as integrating more plant-based meals into our diets, we not only nourish ourselves but also tend to the Earth. Consideration transcends the moment of satiating hunger; each bite becomes a silent statement of support for sustainable practices. It's not merely about forgoing meat, but embracing an entire ecosystem of change—food that demands less water, less land, and induces lower greenhouse gas emissions. This chapter seeks to digest the imperative role mindful eating plays in sculpting a future that is tenable for both humanity and the habitats that surround us, without delving into the detailed strategies reserved for subsequent sections.

## The Impact of Meat Consumption

As our journey into the intricate relationship between our daily practices and the environment continues, it becomes essential to examine one of the most impactful aspects of our lives: our diet. The food choices we make have far-reaching implications for the planet, touching on issues as diverse as resource allocation, greenhouse gas emissions, and biodiversity. Particularly, the consumption of meat plays a pivotal role in this dynamic, shaping ecosystems and influencing climate patterns on a global scale.

Meat production stands as one of the most resource-intensive industries. To begin with, consider the sheer amount of water required for livestock farming. It takes thousands of gallons of water to produce just one pound of beef, a figure that dwarfs the water footprint of plant-based foods. Such heavy water usage exacerbates the strain on our already overtaxed freshwater resources, compounding the challenges of water scarcity around the world.

Moreover, the land demands of meat production are staggering. Vast tracts of forest land are cleared to provide pasture for cattle and to cultivate feed crops, leading to deforestation and habitat destruction. This land-use change not only diminishes the planet's capacity to absorb carbon dioxide but also results in the loss of biodiversity, stripping the earth of its natural resilience to environmental stresses.

When it comes to greenhouse gases, the livestock sector is a significant contributor. Methane, a potent greenhouse gas, is released by ruminant animals, such as cows, during digestion. This methane has a warming potential considerably greater than carbon dioxide over a 20-year period, making the emissions from livestock farming a critical factor in understanding the industry's climate change implications.

Animal agriculture also contributes to the pollution of waterways through runoff laden with fertilizers, antibiotics, and animal waste. These pollutants can lead to eutrophication, creating dead zones in aquatic ecosystems where life can no longer be sustained. This degradation is not limited to local environments but has repercussions that ripple throughout the environmental fabric of our world.

The use of antibiotics in meat production has given rise to additional concerns, particularly the emergence of antibiotic-resistant bacteria. As these organisms find their way into the broader environment, they pose a severe health threat to human populations, complicating infections that were once readily treatable with standard antibiotics.

With the global population continuing to rise, and the demand for meat along with it, the current trends in meat consumption are simply not sustainable. The inefficiency of calorie conversion from feed to meat entails a significant loss of potential energy, a luxury we can ill afford when considering the pressing need to feed a growing world in more sustainable ways.

It becomes clear that personal dietary choices can reverberate through the environmental system, influencing factors as far-reaching as climate patterns and species survival. Shifting to a diet lower in meat can dramatically reduce one's ecological footprint, as plant-based foods generally require fewer resources to produce and result in lower emissions.

The challenge before us is not insubstantial, but neither is it beyond our capabilities. By making informed decisions about what we put on our plates, we can enact change that will fan outwards, touching everything from local ecosystems to the atmosphere encircling our planet. Embracing a plant-forward diet is a transformation that not only benefits personal health but is also a profound act of stewardship for our world.

Additionally, the implications of meat consumption extend into the realm of human equity and social justice. In many parts of the world, grains that could feed people are instead diverted to livestock production. This redirection heightens the paradox of a world where hunger and obesity often coexist—a clear indication that our current food systems are misaligned with global needs.

There is, however, a growing awareness of the need for change, a sentiment that is echoed in the rising popularity of meatless diets and the proliferation of plant-based alternatives. Innovation in food technology is continually providing new ways to enjoy the flavors and textures we desire, with a fraction of the environmental impact.

It is a time for reflection and, more importantly, for action. Each meal provides an opportunity for us to opt for choices that align with a vision of sustainability and environmental harmony. Mindful eating transcends mere nourishment; it becomes an act of engagement with the planet, a daily recommitment to its health and longevity.

While effecting change at the individual level is critical, addressing meat consumption also requires shifts in policy and industry practices. As consumers, our collective demand can drive a transition toward more sustainable meat production methods, encouraging practices that are less resource-intensive, utilize regenerative farming techniques, and prioritize animal welfare.

In conclusion, the impact of meat consumption on our planet is both profound and multifaceted. Each choice to limit meat intake and embrace plant-based options is a step towards a brighter environmental future. By understanding the significance of these choices, we hold the key to unlocking a more sustainable, equitable world where the relationship between humanity and the earth is marked not by exploitation, but by balance and mutual respect.

As we turn the page on outdated habits, let us savor the opportunity to cultivate a legacy of conscious consumption. Our plates have the potential to be canvases of change—a collection of decisions that, when woven together, can help chart a course to a thriving planet. The impact of meat consumption is substantial, yet it is within our collective power to reshape this narrative, meal by mindful meal.

## Embracing Plant-Based Meals

In the dialogue concerning our planet's wellbeing, the foods we choose to consume play a pivotal role. Embracing plant-based meals isn't merely a dietary preference—it is an intentional act of environmental stewardship. When we dive into mindful eating for the planet, we must give considerable thought to the cultivation, distribution, and preparation of our food, particularly regarding the heavy toll of meat consumption on environmental resources.

Plant-based diets are inherently lower in environmental impact compared to diets high in animal products. The water footprint of plant-based food is often drastically lower, for instance. To grow a pound of lentils, considerably less water is needed than to produce the same weight in beef. This disparity draws attention to the significant conservation potential that lies within the plates set before us.

The greenhouse gas emissions connected to plant-based diets are also commendably lower. Animal agriculture is a major contributor to methane and nitrous oxide, both potent greenhouse gases. By shifting towards meals rich in vegetables, grains, fruits, and legumes, each of us can reduce the overall emissions linked to our diet.

Moreover, embracing plant-based meals can lead to a reduction in land use. Vast tracts of land are utilized for grazing or to grow feed for livestock, leading to deforestation and loss of biodiversity. Adopting a plant-based diet means supporting agricultural practices that are more harmonious with nature, preserving habitats, and maintaining ecological balance.

Transitioning to plant-based meals need not be an all-or-nothing approach. Even modest changes, such as participating in Meatless Mondays or choosing plant-based options more frequently during the week, can add up to significant environmental benefits over time. The goal is not to impose a rigid diet but to encourage an evolution towards a more sustainable way of eating.

Plant-based meals also hold the promise of improved health for those who embrace them. An array of studies has tied the consumption of animal products to various health concerns, while a diet rich in plants is often associated with a reduced risk of chronic diseases. It's an alignment of personal health and planetary health that cannot be overlooked.

Furthermore, the variety in plant-based cuisine is astounding. The global tapestry of cultures offers a multitude of dishes that are rich in flavor and nutrition, without relying on meat. Discovering these dishes can expand one's palate and appreciation for the world's cuisines, making the journey to more mindful consumption a delicious one.

Preparing plant-based meals can be simple and time-efficient, an essential consideration for the busy individual. Many plant ingredients require less prep time than meat and can be easily incorporated into quick and nourishing meals. One can start with familiar recipes, substituting plant-based proteins like beans or tempeh, and gradually explore more creative, plant-centered dishes.

Accessibility and affordability are important facets of sustainable eating habits. Plant-based proteins such as beans, lentils, and chickpeas are often more economical than meat, which can be beneficial for household budgets. These staple items can be stored for long periods, reducing food waste and the frequent need to shop, contributing to a lower carbon footprint from transportation.

Embracing plant-based meals also encourages local economies and seasonal eating. Farmers' markets and community-supported agriculture programs often offer a wide range of plant-based foods that support local farmers and minimize the food miles associated with long-distance transportation of goods.

Education is a cornerstone of adopting any new habit, including the incorporation of plant-based meals. Understanding the nutritional content of plant foods can ensure a balanced diet, especially with regard to obtaining enough protein, vitamins, and minerals. This knowledge is power—it empowers consumers to make choices that are good for them and the planet.

When we discuss environmental sustainability, awareness of the need for sustainable food systems is escalating. Our food choices have the potential to either exacerbate or alleviate environmental issues. The embrace of plant-based meals sends a clear message to food producers and retailers that there is a demand for sustainable and ethical options.

Finally, celebrating the act of cooking and eating as a communal and conscientious activity embodies the spirit of mindful eating for the planet. Sharing plant-based meals with friends and family can spread awareness and inspire others to consider the implications of their food choices.

As we consider the paths that lay before us in saving our ailing earth, let us not underestimate the power that lies in the collective adoption of plant-based meals. While the act of choosing a plant-based meal may seem inconsequential in isolation, our individual choices contribute to a larger, collective impact on the environmental health of our planet. It is a conscious choice that we can all make, one plate at a time, towards nurturing and restoring the delicate balance of the world around us.

In embracing plant-based meals, we engage in a daily practice that respects the finitude of our resources and honors our responsibility to future generations. This section lingered on the enduring question of how we feed ourselves sustainably. The following chapters shall open up further discussions on how we can continue to forge a lifestyle that harmonizes with the rhythms of our natural world, with insights into the circular economies of secondhand shopping and the joys of upcycling. Join us as we further explore the many ways in which we can cultivate a greener legacy—one choice at a time.

# Chapter 10:
# The World of Secondhand

Having explored mindful eating in the previous chapter, we delve now into the world of secondhand, a realm where the old becomes new and the discarded finds renewed purpose. In a society often obsessed with the latest and shiniest, there exists an underappreciated avenue for conservation: the secondhand market. Here, we find not only a treasure trove of unique items, each with its own history and character, but also a practical tool to mitigate the relentless cycle of production and waste. Items that could have ended up in landfills are given a second life, reducing the demand on raw materials and energy needed for manufacturing new goods. We are consistently finding that secondhand isn't just a choice for the thrifty, but a purposeful decision for those vigilant in safeguarding our environmental future. Therefore, investigating the ecological and economic virtues of thrift stores, garage sales, and online marketplaces becomes more than just a savvy shopping strategy—it's an integral aspect of an eco-conscious lifestyle that celebrates the value lingering within the pre-loved.

## Shopping Smart: Thrifts and Swaps

In our journey toward a more sustainable existence, the choices we make in our consumption habits play a critical role. As we turn the pages in the book of eco-conscious living, the section on thrift stores and swap meets emerges as a beacon of hope and pragmatism in the quest for a kinder approach to our planet's resources. Let's unravel the benefits of embracing secondhand shopping and how it forms an essential component of a greener lifestyle.

Trendy thrift stores and swap events are not just a nostalgic nod to bygone eras; they're a smart, eco-friendly solution to modern consumerism's toll on the planet. With the fashion industry being one of the major contributors to waste and pollution, turning to these secondhand sources helps reduce the demand for new products and the associated environmental impacts of production and disposal.

Thrift shopping allows items to have prolonged lifetimes, slowing the relentless churn of resources needed to produce new goods. It's not merely about saving money; it's a form of protest against the wastefulness that pervades our culture. Every garment picked from a thrift store rack or a pre-loved book carried home stands as a testament to the value inherent in reusing and appreciating what already exists.

Participating in clothing swap events is another powerful way to diminish clothing waste. Today's unwanted shirt or dress becomes tomorrow's cherished find for someone else, fostering a community of shared values and collective responsibility. Imagine a world where clothes rotate through cycles of ownership, appreciated by one person after another. Swaps make this idyllic vision a tangible reality.

Moreover, thrifts and swaps offer a unique variety that mainstream shopping can't match. Vintage finds and eclectic pieces tell stories, exude character, and allow personal style to flourish without the carbon footprint that comes with fast fashion. They provide an opportunity for consumers to express individuality while aligning their actions with their concern for the planet.

However, smart thrifting doesn't just happen; it requires a discerning eye. Quality over quantity remains a mantra for sustainable living. It's crucial to look for well-made items that will stand the test of time, rather than succumbing to the transient allure of low-cost items that will soon require replacement.

Accessibility is another virtue of thrift stores and swaps. They offer a low-pressure environment to learn about environmentally conscious living at one's own pace. This approach can be particularly impactful for those just starting their green journey, providing a gentle entry point without the overwhelm that sometimes accompanies major lifestyle overhauls.

Let's not forget the community aspect. These secondhand hubs often serve as meeting grounds for like-minded individuals who share a common goal of sustainability. They're places where ideas and lessons on living green can flow as freely as the goods themselves, nurturing bonds over shared values.

An often-overlooked advantage of thrifting and swapping is the reduction of packaging waste. Unlike new products, which often come excessively packaged in plastic and other materials, secondhand items require no such excess. This simple yet impactful difference helps to further lessen the volume of waste destined for landfills or incinerators.

For the uninitiated, the process of shopping at thrift stores and participating in swaps might seem daunting at first. Yet, most find that the thrill of the hunt and the joy of discovery quickly overshadow any initial hesitations. To aid in integrating these practices, one might begin by identifying specific needs before attending a swap or visiting a thrift shop, which can provide a sense of direction and intent.

The environmental merits of these practices are significant, but they also carry social value. Thrifting and swapping often support charitable organizations and local communities. Money spent at non-profit thrift stores frequently goes toward local services and initiatives, thus your purchases can support more than just a sustainable wardrobe; they can uplift your community.

Advocating for the secondhand market also sends a message to corporations about consumer priorities. As more people choose used goods, businesses notice the shift and may adjust their practices accordingly. In essence, thrifting and swapping can drive systemic change through collective consumer behavior.

Children, too, can benefit from early exposure to thrifts and swaps. Engaging young minds in these sustainable practices fosters a natural inclination towards eco-friendly choices and sets the stage for them to become responsible stewards of the Earth as they mature.

The obstacles that hinder the pursuit of a sustainable lifestyle are numerous, but the solutions reside in our daily actions. The adoption of secondhand shopping is a potent tool in the arsenal against the environmental crisis. It's a choice that manifests conscientious living without forsaking the pleasures of personal expression and style.

As we close the chapter on thrifts and swaps, remember that each minor decision cascades into a major impact. This section has illuminated how embracing the secondhand world is not just an act of frugality; it's a commitment to the future of our planet, blending the wisdom of conservation with the brilliance of modern mindfulness. Thrifts and swaps are more than just a trend; they are a transformational movement towards a more harmonic existence with the Earth. A movement that you are now a part of.

## The Joys of Upcycling

The world of secondhand doesn't just end at thrifting or swapping; it blooms with limitless potential through the process of upcycling. Transforming unwanted products into new, useful or aesthetically pleasing items not only gives these objects a second chance at life but also mitigates the ever-growing issue of waste polluting our shared planet.

Upcycling is an art form as much as it is an environmental stance, blending creativity with ecological consciousness. Every upcycled piece tells a distinct story, reflects individuality, and showcases the ingenuity of the human spirit in its quest for sustainability. The joy of transforming the old into new is a celebration of resourcefulness and embodies the mantra of reduced consumption.

When you upcycle, you take part in a quiet revolution against the single-use culture. It's a powerful stand to decrease the number of items that end up in landfills, where they contribute to methane emissions and take up valuable space. The challenge of creating something valuable from the rejected is a voyage of discovery, where one person's trash indeed becomes another's treasure.

In the act of upcycling, materials that would have otherwise contributed to pollution gain a new purpose. Fabric scraps turn into beautiful quilts, wooden pallets become elegant furniture, and old glass jars morph into stylish light fixtures. Each transformed item not only removes waste from our ecosystem but also negates the need for new resources to be consumed.

Let's not forget the economic benefits that accompany upcycling. By repurposing materials, you can save money that would have been spent on new items. Crafting unique home decorations or fashion pieces from upcycled goods can lead to significant cost savings, which is a welcome advantage in today's economy.

Moreover, upcycling fosters a deeper appreciation for materials and their potential to be repurposed. It encourages us to look at items not just for what they are but for what they could become. This perspective shift is vital in cultivating a mentality of conservation and respect towards the resources our planet provides.

The process of upcycling also supports local communities. By sourcing materials from local thrift stores or flea markets, you contribute to the circular economy where goods and materials are kept in use for as long as possible, thus providing community jobs and reducing environmental impact.

One cannot overlook the educational aspect of upcycling. It serves as a hands-on teaching tool for all ages, demonstrating practically the core principles of sustainability. Through workshops and DIY projects, upcycling can enlighten individuals on the importance of environmental stewardship and inspire them to act.

As we witness climate change's effects growing more severe, upcycling signifies hope and progress. It represents a proactive, can-do attitude towards making a tangible difference, no matter the scale. The message is clear: we all have the power to enact change through our daily actions and choices.

Furthermore, upcycling feeds into the broader narrative of sustainable living. It compliments other green practices like recycling, composting, and water conservation by falling perfectly into the eco-friendly lifestyle many strive to adopt. In essence, it's a keystroke in the symphony of sustainability that our planet urgently needs us to play.

The joy of upcycling lies also in its community aspect. Sharing before-and-after pictures of upcycled projects on social media, participating in local upcycling events, or joining online forums sparks conversations and encouragement amongst like-minded individuals. These interactions lead to a sense of belonging in a community dedicated to making a difference.

Every upcycled item sends a message to manufacturers as well. It underscores the demand for more sustainable, long-lasting products and calls for an end to planned obsolescence. Upcycling is a feedback mechanism, telling the market that sustainability is not only preferred but demanded by consumers.

Most importantly, the joy of upcycling is deeply personal. Each project, be it small or large, is a step towards an environmentally conscious lifestyle. It's a testament to one's dedication to preserving this planet for future generations. The satisfaction derived from crafting a one-of-a-kind item is unparalleled, especially when it aligns with the values of sustainability.

In conclusion, upcycling is a multifaceted gem in the world of secondhand that enriches our lives and environment. It's a tangible, joyful pursuit that resonates with the need for sustainable practices in our daily routines. It's not only about saving items from waste; it's about preserving the essence of our planet, one creative project at a time.

As we venture forward, let us remember that upcycling is more than just a pastime. It's a critical component of our collective effort to heal the earth. Engaging in the joys of upcycling is not merely enjoyable; it's a vital, transformative act that reverberates hope and change for the very fabric of our world.

# Chapter 11:
# Advocating for Change

As we weave through the rich tapestry of efforts to preserve our precious planet, the narrative brings us to a crucial pivot point: the power of our collective voice in advocating for change. With the relentless workings of time, small actions have shown their might, yet a transformative tide requires us to step into the arena of environmental policy. This chapter introduces the art of engaging civically, of wielding the pen and the protest with equal fervor. Understanding how to support and push for eco-friendly legislation isn't just a rallying cry—it's a demonstration of the deep-seated commitment we share in safeguarding our earth's future. Here, the focus shifts to the sphere where policy shapes practice, where the individual's call for sustainability becomes the chorus that leads to legislative landmarks. Empowerment stems from knowledge, from discerning the mechanisms that drive environmental decisions at the governmental level and tailoring our actions to make the substantial impacts that the times so desperately require.

## Engaging with Environmental Policy

Transitioning from individual actions to broader societal change requires a keen understanding of the interconnected mechanisms that shape our environment. While personal choices are vital, policy and legislation reflect the frameworks within which those choices are made. Engaging with environmental policy is not only about advocating for change but also about understanding the levers of power and influence that can protect and restore our planet.

Policy engagement begins with education. Citizens must acquaint themselves with the existing environmental statutes, regulations, and guidelines that govern their localities, regions, and the nation. This knowledge base is essential, as it equips you with the understanding necessary to critique, support, or call for modifications to those policies.

The legislative process may seem daunting but participating in public hearings, comment periods, and town hall meetings is a tangible method of influence. These forums are designed to gather input from stakeholders—namely, the community—which means your voice is not only welcome but also legally significant.

Relationships with elected representatives can yield considerable influence over environmental policy. Regular communication with local council members, state legislators, or national representatives, ideally through a mix of in-person meetings, phone calls, and written correspondence, can establish you as a concerned and active constituent.

Voting is a pivotal act of civic engagement. By supporting candidates with robust environmental platforms, the electorate signals the demand for stronger environmental stewardship from their leaders. Research the environmental records and commitments of those running for office and exercise your democratic right to support those who align with sustainable values.

Lobbying, once a term reserved for professional advocates, has become a grassroots activity in many communities. Collaborating with environmental groups to meet with officials or send targeted messages is an effective tactic that amplifies the call for specific policy prescriptions.

Empowerment often comes through coalition-building, where unity with like-minded individuals and organizations can create a formidable force for change. Becoming an active member of environmentally focused groups not only offers camaraderie but also represents a collective that cannot be easily ignored by policymakers.

The intricacies of environmental legislation can be complex, with nuances often buried within legal jargon. Hence, collaboration with environmental lawyers and policy experts can help to demystify proposals, interpret potential impacts, and craft cogent arguments against or for certain policies.

Media engagement can sway public opinion and, by extension, influence policy. Writing op-eds, letters to the editor, and using social platforms to discuss and promote sustainable policies are modern strategies to spread awareness and catalyze action among the broader populace.

Staying informed about international agreements and initiatives, such as the Paris Agreement, is immensely beneficial. Global policies often trickle down to national and local legislation, and understanding these can inspire local advocacy efforts that align with or push against these international commitments.

To truly engage with environmental policy, there must be a determined and proactive investment in continuous learning. The field is dynamic, with policies constantly evolving in response to new research, technology, and the growing urgency of environmental challenges.

Active participation may also involve submitting written proposals for policy adjustments or new legislation. With expert assistance or through collective brainstorming with environmental groups, citizens can delineate potential solutions to environmental concerns that lawmakers may overlook.

When engaging in environmental policy, it's imperative to frame arguments in a manner that resonates across ideological divides. Highlight economic benefits, such as job creation through green energy, or invoke the universal desire for clean air and water to garner wider support for environmental policies.

Effective policy engagement also hinges on accountability. Monitor the outcomes of legislation and ensure that implementation matches intent. Hold representatives and authorities responsible if policies are not enforced or if results are not meeting community or scientific standards.

Finally, recognize that while policy work can be slow and full of setbacks, it's through persistence and collective pressure that long-term environmental protection is achieved. Through informed, motivated, and patient involvement, our voices can drive the change necessary to steer our society toward sustainability and the preservation of our planet for generations to come.

**How to Support Eco-Friendly Legislation** Within the tide of environmental advocacy, supporting eco-friendly legislation is akin to planting seeds of change at a systemic level. The lifeblood of this advocacy lies in engaging with the policy that sets the stage for a sustainable future. Herein, we explore practical steps an individual can take to help galvanize this vital aspect of environmental activism.

First, awareness is the cornerstone of action. Learning about the legislative process and current environmental bills under consideration can provide invaluable insight. Individuals can track legislation through government websites and environmental advocacy groups' updates. Moreover, signing up for newsletters from environmental organizations can keep one informed about bills to watch and support.

Communication with elected representatives is a powerful tool for change. Whether it's through email, phone calls, or town hall meetings, letting lawmakers know you support or oppose specific legislation makes your voice heard. Personalized messages tend to be more effective than form letters, so take the time to articulate why a certain piece of legislation is important to you and your community.

Public support can often propel a bill's success. Attending rallies, participating in letter-writing campaigns, and encouraging peers through social media can cultivate communal backing. Social platforms are robust arenas for amplifying eco-friendly initiatives; each post shared can ripple outwards, garnering more attention and endorsement.

Furthermore, utilizing voter power is indispensable. Supporting candidates who prioritize the environment can lead to the passage of progressive policies. Your vote is a commitment to environmental stewardship and should align with candidates who demonstrate genuine ecological consideration.

Volunteering for campaigns that support eco-friendly legislation also amplifies its potential impact. Whether it's canvassing, phone banking, or organizing community events, your hands-on involvement can make a tangible difference. Harness the synergy of collaboration by teaming up with others who share the same passion for the planet.

Penning op-eds or letters to the editor in local newspapers can also extend the reach of your advocacy. An articulate and poignant piece about the necessity of a certain bill can inform and inspire readers, potentially influencing public opinion and lawmakers' decisions.

Financial contributions, even those that are modest, can also bolster the resources of those fighting for the environment at the legislative level. Campaigns, non-profits, and advocacy groups often rely on donations to keep their operations afloat and their missions moving forward.

Education and dialogue can be just as crucial as financial contributions. Initiating conversations with family, friends, and neighbors about the importance of supporting eco-friendly laws fosters a culture of consciousness around environmental issues. Knowledge shared is potential action garnered.

Lastly, consistent advocacy is vital for enduring change. Engage with legislation beyond immediate crises or hot-button issues.

Continuous support for environmental causes strengthens the persistence required to shift policies toward a more sustainable paradigm.

In summation, a myriad of paths lay open for those eager to support eco-friendly legislation. Each step taken, however small it may seem, threads into the larger quilt of collective action. From understanding to engagement, and from ballots to blogs, every facet of participation is a stride towards the environmental ethos we strive to achieve. Remember, individual actions, when aggregated, wield the power to transform the political landscape and secure a more verdant and viable world for generations to come.

# Chapter 12:
# Building a Green Community

The idea of a greener future is increasingly vital, bringing us to the imperative discussion on building sustainable communities. It's clear that individually we can make ripples, but collectively, we can make waves in the quest for environmental stewardship. This chapter explores the pragmatic steps to foster an eco-conscious society—a harmonization of economy and ecology. It delves into the significance of local initiatives, the power vested in group efforts, and how to synergize into a cohesive green movement. Our exploration addresses how to implement strategies that not only mitigate our environmental footprint but also strengthen community bonds. We'll reveal the transformative influence of cooperative gardens, energy co-ops, and innovative recycling programs, which demonstrate how a community can thrive while adhering to principles of sustainability. The tenets laid out here are a blueprint for action, depicting how joint commitment can construct a resilient framework for our neighborhoods to confront the environmental challenges of our times.

## Local Initiatives and Group Efforts

As we delve into the fabric of creating a sustainable community, we can't overlook the power of local initiatives and group efforts. Collaboration is the cornerstone of environmental stewardship, allowing individuals to magnify their impact through collective action. These local endeavors, often sparked by a small group of committed citizens, have the capability of initiating profound change within communities.

Local initiatives often address specific environmental issues that residents face. This targeted approach can lead to the implementation of community gardens that provide fresh, local produce while educating residents on sustainable agriculture. Such initiatives serve a dual role, both reducing the carbon footprint associated with transporting food and reinforcing the bond amongst the community members.

Group efforts furthermore tend to foster environmental education. Workshops and seminars led by local experts on topics like reducing plastic use or creating pollinator-friendly landscapes serve as communal learning experiences. Access to knowledge empowers residents to make informed decisions, which leads to a stronger, more resilient green community.

A shining example of collective impact is the establishment of farmer's markets. These markets not only support regional agriculture but also minimize waste through reduced packaging and shorter supply chains. They act as a nucleus for the community, offering a platform where ideas and products in alignment with environmental consciousness are exchanged.

Neighborhood clean-up events are yet another symbol of the strength found in unity. By organizing river, beach, or park clean-ups, communities can visibly enhance their local environment, which often inspires ongoing stewardship and pride in their natural surroundings. Such events can also draw media attention, further spreading awareness and encouraging broader participation.

Community-wide recycling drives are immensely effective as well. They provide an avenue for responsible disposal of items like electronics or hazardous materials, which might otherwise end up in landfills. These initiatives not only remove waste but also educate the public on the importance of proper waste segregation and recycling.

On the cutting edge of environmental activism are renewable energy co-ops. These cooperatives give community members the chance to invest in renewable energy projects, reducing dependence on fossil fuels and leading the transition to a sustainable future. Such projects also serve as a tangible symbol of a community's commitment to environmental stewardship.

Local initiatives extend into the realm of transportation as well. Car-sharing programs reduce the number of vehicles on the road, decreasing emissions and traffic congestion. Similarly, campaigns to improve cycling infrastructure promote cleaner air and healthier lifestyles.

Urban green spaces, facilitated by collaborations between residents and local governments, are oases in the concrete jungle. These spaces contribute not only to the aesthetic appeal of a city but also to the mental and physical well-being of its inhabitants, all the while enhancing biodiversity.

School-based projects carry the message of sustainability to younger generations. These programs often include the installation of solar panels on school roofs, the creation of educational gardens, or the implementation of recycling programs, instilling a sense of environmental responsibility in students early on.

Innovation through local programs can also lead to significant advancements. Many communities have seen the advent of tool-lending libraries, which reduce the need for individual ownership of infrequently used items, promoting a sharing economy and reducing material consumption.

Citizen science projects encourage community members to become researchers in their own right. By collecting data on local flora and fauna or participating in water quality monitoring, residents contribute to scientific understanding and the management of local environmental health.

Tree planting initiatives in cities and suburbs are a direct way to combat the urban heat island effect and sequester carbon dioxide. Groups of neighbors coming together to plant trees is not just an ecological act; it's an affirmation of the community's commitment to fostering life and shade for future generations.

Efforts to promote sustainable local businesses also play a critical role. By choosing to support businesses that have adopted eco-friendly practices, community members incentivize green innovation and the circular economy. This patronage completes a vital feedback loop that encourages other businesses to follow suit.

In conclusion, it's clear that local initiatives and group efforts create ripples that can expand into waves of environmental consciousness and action. Each undertaking builds upon another, leading to a robust network of environmentally-minded individuals and groups. It's within these collaborations that we find the hope and determination for building a sustainable future - a future in which every community shines as a beacon of green unity, inspiring others to do the same.

**Starting a Green Movement in Your Area** As stewards of our environment, it's imperative to recognize the influential power of community action. If you've felt the need to foster a green transformation within your neighborhood or town, you're already on the right path. Activating a grassroots movement can be a powerful catalyst for sustainable change, one that resonates deeply within the local populace and engenders a collective consciousness towards environmental stewardship.

Embarking on this endeavor begins with education. Knowledge is a precursory step to enacting change. Gather data and resources that highlight pressing environmental issues pertinent to your area. This could involve problems like local pollution, deforestation, waste management, or water quality. Hold informative meetings or workshops to spread awareness, making use of engaging formats and reliable research to illustrate the urgency of these predicaments and their potential solutions.

Collaboration is the cornerstone of any movement. Reach out to like-minded individuals, local businesses, schools, and community groups to form an alliance. Diverse backgrounds will bring a plethora of skills, ideas, and resources to the table. Develop a clear mission statement and set of goals that align with the unique needs and characteristics of your locality. This provides a shared vision and framework for action that all participants can rally around.

Visibility is key to maintaining momentum. Create a brand for your movement with a memorable name and logo, and use social media platforms to engage a wider audience. Regular updates on progress, events, and success stories will keep participants informed and inspired. Moreover, this increased visibility can attract new members who wish to contribute to the cause.

Inspiration often stems from action. Organize events and initiatives that have tangible impacts, such as neighborhood clean-ups, tree planting days, or implementing recycling programs. These hands-on activities not only improve the local environment but also give participants a sense of accomplishment and an illustrative example of what can be achieved through collective effort.

Fundraising is essential for sustaining any movement. Consider hosting events, like charity runs, silent auctions, or local fairs, where proceeds go directly towards environmental projects or education. Seek out grants and sponsorships from organizations that are aligned with your goals. Sustainable funding will enable your group to undertake larger projects and have a more profound influence within the community.

Engagement with local governance cannot be overstated. Present your mission and findings to municipal leaders and persuade them to implement greener policies or invest in sustainable community projects. It's not uncommon for local governments to be unaware of the public's demand for environmental consideration. A cohesive movement presents a unified voice that's hard to ignore.

Education must continue beyond the inception of the movement. Plan for the future by establishing educational programs in local schools and libraries, focusing on environmental conservation. Instilling eco-conscious values in the younger generation creates a continuity that ensures the long-term viability of the movement.

As you foster a green community, celebrate every victory, no matter how small. Whether it's a successful event or a strategy that has borne fruit, recognition and celebration keep spirits high. These actions remind everyone involved that their efforts are making a difference. Share testimonials and stories from volunteers or locals who have experienced the positive changes brought by the movement.

To truly thrive, a green movement must be inclusive and adaptable. Encourage feedback and suggestions, continually seeking innovative approaches to environmental challenges. Be open to evolving tactics and strategies as new information and technologies emerge. Adaptability not only strengthens the movement but ensures it remains relevant.

Initiating a green movement in your area is a journey of passion and persistence that can drive remarkable change and foster a more sustainable world. It is the small threads woven by individual communities, such as yours, that reinforce the fabric of a global environmental revolution. Each step taken collectively enriches the health of our planet and echoes the message that the time for action is now.

# Chapter 13:
# A Greener Tomorrow Starts Today

As we conclude the poignant journey through the pages of this guide, we stand at the threshold of change. Our exploration has illuminated the myriad pathways through which each individual's behavior casts ripples upon the waters of the world. These final reflections aim not just to summarize our learned lessons, but to instill a fervent sense of purpose and determination to act—for it's the actions we take today that will sculpt the verdant world of our tomorrows.

Understanding our role in the shaping of Earth's present and future starts with acknowledging the power vested in our everyday choices. Each morsel of food, every drop of water, every purchase, commute, and disposal, paints a stroke on the larger canvas of our planet's health. Grasping that our mundane decisions weave together to form the larger tapestry of global sustainability is vital. It empowers us to make changes that, collectively, can lead to a monumental shift towards environmental equilibrium.

Recycling, as we've discovered, is more than a chore; it's a commitment to renewing life's cycle and respecting the delicate balance of nature. It extends well beyond sorting bins—a vision of ingenuity and conscious consumption. By finding new ways to reuse what we might once have deemed waste, we forge an alliance with the environment, recognizing that the resources we cherish are borrowed, not owned.

Similarly, the magic of composting transforms what might be discarded into nourishing soil, the very bedrock of terrestrial life. This alchemist's act reminds us that death and decay are not mere ends, but the beginnings of new life. As such, we foster a symbiosis with nature, understanding we are not separate from it, but an integral part of its perpetual cycle.

Household waste reduction isn't merely about avoiding single-use items or discovering eco-friendly products; it's fundamentally about mindfulness. A mindfulness that asks us to examine the necessity and the impact of everything that crosses the threshold of our homes. By deliberating on our daily habits and tweaking them gently, we channel an immense capacity for positive change.

Water conservation goes past the turn of a faucet. It's a homage to the precious essence of life, and when we actively work to safeguard each precious drop, we participate in the protection of all life on Earth. It's not only a matter of fixing leaks but embracing a philosophy that values and sustains the life forces that flow around and within us.

Investigating the carbon footprint left behind by our footsteps and the tires of our vehicles reveals an opportunity. An opportunity to choose alternatives—like biking, walking, or public transit—that minimize our impact and demonstrate a respect for the purity of air, the openness of skies, and the health of all who breathe within it.

The stewardship of energy extends into the sanctity of our homes, subtly intertwined with the choices we make in appliances and everyday electricity usage. To be energy efficient is to be an ally of the future, safeguarding the atmosphere and the climate that envelops our shared world.

We have delved into the plates on our tables, understanding that each bite of food carries with it the story of its journey to us—the water, land, and energy consumed. Embracing plant-based meals becomes an act of compassion, not just for the animals but for the environment that sustains all creatures, great and small.

The allure of secondhand markets, the joyous discovery of thrifting and upcycling, unveils a realm where objects are imbued with extended life. Here, we celebrate the virtue of reimagining, of giving a second chance—values that echo in the chambers of our collective conscience and whisper the promise of sustainability.

Indeed, advocacy stretches far beyond our personal sphere—it touches the realm of policy, where voices united can steer the grand ship of state towards conservation and care for our natural world. Active engagement in environmental legislation is no longer a choice but a profound responsibility.

A green community is the sum of its individuals, each contributing their unique hue to the vibrant mosaic of environmental action. Starting a local movement, participating in initiatives, or simply joining with others in a collective effort magnifies our capacity to make a meaningful, lasting impact.

Our explorations conclude, but the journey never truly ends. We stand on the precipice of tomorrow, gazing forward with wisdom gleaned and resolutions steeled. It is imperative that we seize this moment with both hands, recognizing the responsibility bestowed upon us—guardians of a planet that yearns for our empathy and our action.

Therefore, let us not part ways without acknowledging the monumental task ahead, nor without the confidence that each step we take is a stride toward a greener tomorrow. By imbuing our lives with conscious choices, an ethos of preservation, and a pledge to do no harm, we set into motion the forces of change. And it is within this dedication, this daily commitment to a living, breathing planet, that we find hope and the very essence of our continued existence.

Let the words etched upon these pages not echo into the void but resonate through our actions and our lives. May our aspirations for a greener tomorrow begin not in some distant future, but here, now, today, within us all. For in the end, it is our collective efforts, compiled from single, small actions, that hold the power to shape our destiny and bestow upon the next generations a world abundant and thriving. A greener tomorrow, indeed, starts today.

# Appendix A:
# Further Reading and Resources

The journey we've embarked on together doesn't conclude with the closing of these pages. The quest for a sustainable planet is relentless and requires a continuous influx of knowledge and inspiration. Within this appendix lie gateways to a deeper understanding—a curated collection of readings and resources that endeavor to supplement your commitment to this cause.

## Books

*The Uninhabitable Earth: Life After Warming* by David Wallace-Wells — An exploration of the profound changes our planet will undergo in the decades to come due to climate change.

*This Changes Everything: Capitalism vs. The Climate* by Naomi Klein — A compelling argument about the economic structures that need to evolve to avert climate crisis.

*Drawdown: The Most Comprehensive Plan Ever Proposed to Reverse Global Warming* edited by Paul Hawken — A solution-focused approach presenting the most effective actions to combat climate change.

## Online Resources

The Intergovernmental Panel on Climate Change (IPCC) — The United Nations body for assessing the science related to climate change, providing essential reports and data.

Project Drawdown (drawdown.org) — A research organization that reviews, analyzes, and identifies the most viable global climate solutions.

Environmental Working Group (ewg.org) — A resource for understanding everyday impacts on the environment and how to minimize them in your personal choices.

## Documentaries and Films

*An Inconvenient Truth* and *An Inconvenient Sequel: Truth to Power* — Al Gore's influential documentaries focusing on the perils of climate change and his campaign to address it.

*Chasing Coral* — A film that vividly showcases the existential threat to our world's coral reefs due to warming oceans.

*Before the Flood* — A documentary that paints a stark picture of the impact humans have had on the environment, narrated by Leonardo DiCaprio.

## Podcasts

*How to Save a Planet* — Co-hosted by journalist Alex Blumberg and scientist Dr. Ayana Elizabeth Johnson, this podcast questions what it means to preserve the environment and offers practical advice and stories.

*The Climate Question* from BBC World Service — Offers insightful discussions on how climate change affects our world and diverse perspectives on how people are responding globally.

*Mothers of Invention* — Fronted by former Irish President Mary Robinson and comedian Maeve Higgins, this podcast showcases women around the world who are leaders in climate innovation and justice.

Let this reading list serve as a fertile ground for your expanding consciousness and as a testament to the copious work done by writers, filmmakers, scientists, and activists in informing and shaping public discourse. Whether you're scribbling notes, lending your voice to a cause, or fostering growth within your community—you're not alone in this. By furthering your education, you're harnessing the potential to enact change on a scalable and profoundly personal level, ensuring that with each step forward, we're collectively nurturing a more resilient and thriving planet for future generations.

# Appendix B:
# Quick Reference Guide for Earth-Friendly Living

As we journey through the multifaceted roles we play in the stewardship of our planet, it becomes apparent that every individual stride in an eco-conscious direction is pivotal. The path toward a sustainable future is paved with the aggregate of our daily decisions. The world demands considerate and deliberate action, grounded in a profound respect for the natural systems that sustain us. This quick-reference guide is tailored to assist you in embedding Earth-friendly practices into the rhythm of your everyday life.

## 1. Smart Shopping Choices

**Buy in Bulk:** Purchasing bulk items reduces packaging waste and often saves money.

**Reusable Bags:** Always carry a reusable bag to mitigate the pollution from plastic ones.

**Conscious Consumerism:** Support brands and businesses committed to sustainability.

## 2. Home Habits

**Energy Conservation:** Unplug appliances when not in use and invest in energy-efficient ones. LED bulbs can make a significant difference.

**Eco-Friendly Products:** Choose household cleaners that are non-toxic and biodegradable.

**Zero Waste Practices:** Embrace reusable items, like cloth napkins and beeswax wraps, over their disposable counterparts.

## 3. Waste Reduction

**Compost:** Turn your organic kitchen waste into nutrient-rich compost for your garden.

**Recycle Properly:** Follow local guidelines to ensure your recyclables are processed correctly.

**Upcycle:** Before disposal, consider if an item can have a second life through creativity.

## 4. Sustainable Nutrition

**Plant-Based Choices:** Incorporate more vegetarian and vegan meals into your diet to reduce your carbon footprint.

**Local and Seasonal:** Purchase from farmers' markets to support local agriculture and reduce transportation emissions.

**Minimize Food Waste:** Plan meals and store food correctly to avoid unnecessary spoilage.

## 5. Water Conservation

**Fix Leaks:** Small drips can lead to substantial water loss over time. Addressing them promptly conserves water.

**Water-Saving Fixtures:** Install low-flow toilets and showerheads to reduce water usage.

**Conscious Use:** Be mindful of water use while washing dishes, showering, and watering plants.

## 6. Transportation

**Carpool or Public Transit:** Share rides or use public transportation to cut down on individual vehicle emissions.

**Cycling and Walking:** Opt for these zero-emission modes of transport for short distances.

**Vehicle Maintenance:** Regular tune-ups ensure your vehicle operates more efficiently and with lower emissions.

## 7. Community Involvement

**Local Initiatives:** Support or start local environmental projects like tree planting or clean-up drives.

**Education:** Share knowledge and resources on sustainable practices with family, friends, and neighbors.

**Policy Advocacy:** Use your voice to advocate for environmentally responsible policies.

The quest for a greener life is ongoing, evolving with our growing understanding of what our planet requires and how best we can answer that call. Even the most cursory glance at these suggestions can reveal opportunities for more sustainable living, and when woven into the fabric of daily life, the cumulative effect can be profound and far-reaching. Embrace this guide as a starting point to a dynamic, everyday commitment to the care of our Earth. It's not the grand gestures but the persistent small actions that engineer the monumental shift toward a more sustainable world.